MW01533674

Endorsements

"At the dawn of the Twentieth Century, Theodore Roosevelt warned us of the dangers of educating intellect, while neglecting soul. The era now ending, full of both tragedy and hope, witnessed the truth of TR's comment. Dr. Robert Kamm's new book calls us back to "the best of mind and spirit." Perhaps suffering humanity can find, as Aleksandr Solzhenitsyn hoped in his 1978 commencement address at Harvard University, a new era that sustains prosperity without smothering our fundamental spiritual nature. Let Bob Kamm, an educator and a man of faith, lead the way."

—Patrick B. McGuigan, Editor of the Editorial Page
The Daily Oklahoman
Oklahoma City, OK

"*The Best of Mind and Spirit* is a rare work due to the expressions from the heart of a respected academician who understands from personal experience the potential of a human being who has nurtured both the intellect and the spirit. The eloquence of thought and the excellent documentation of other sources will make this work an invaluable addition to the libraries of all who are seriously interested in educating human beings to their full potential as endowed by their Creator."

—Dr. Floyd Coppedge, Secretary of Education
State of Oklahoma

"Dr. Kamm recognizes a great but neglected truth—that mankind is primarily a spiritual being, and that any approach to education needs a strong spiritual and moral emphasis and not just a physical dimension. Through his new book, Dr. Kamm has focused on a major problem and issued a major challenge to society."

—William R. Bright, Former President and Founder
Campus Crusade for Christ International
Orlando, FL

"President Kamm converted us from a college into a university by broadening the range of interests and emphases to include the total perspective of an education."

—Dr. Norbert Mahnken, Emeritus Professor of
History, Oklahoma State University
Stillwater, OK
On the occasion of his retirement following
50 years of teaching

"Dr. Kamm furnished the authoritative voice of senior academic leadership in the USA's contribution to the work of the United Nations Educational, Scientific and Cultural Organization's Executive Board. Also, his experiences in UNESCO with those of most nations of the world led him to realize how blessed America is with its comprehensive public education system."

—Russell C. Heater, Director for UNESCO Affairs
Department of State, 1975-1978
Springfield, VA

"Thank you so much for sharing *The Best of Mind and Spirit.* I commend you for your commitment to awakening America's young people to the need for moral goodness, bound together with an understanding of the values that built this country. The issues you discuss are the same issues Oklahoma educators face daily. Your words are reassuring that our country can return to a land of virtue and righteousness."

—Sandy Garrett, Oklahoma State Superintendent
of Public Instruction
Oklahoma City, OK

"I'm so pleased that a man of your stature, ability, and experience would attempt such a marvelous undertaking. All who have opportunity to read your work will be blessed by it. I thank you for being a special friend to my family and to all Americans."

—Dr. Mouzon Biggs, Jr., Sr. Minister
The Boston Avenue Church, United Methodist
Tulsa, OK

Contents

Preface

The United States of America, the world's greatest nation, is in trouble—not so much economically, nor technologically, nor politically as the global leader, but in its decline morally and spiritually.

This is not a volume of gloom and condemnation, as much as it is an expression of hope and faith in the face of disturbing realities—a belief that we as citizens of our great nation will take the essential steps to reverse the present values decline and to get back on the track established by those who founded this nation (and those who labored to bring to fruition the dreams and the vision of our Founders).

I am a first generation American who has been privileged to be involved internationally to a considerable extent through the years. While these experiences abroad have been enjoyed and appreciated, the most meaningful aspects of my experiences abroad have been, first, to come to recognize how much the diverse peoples of the world are really one family; and, second, to gain an ever-increasing appreciation and affection for the United States of America as the land of the free and of continuing opportunity for its people. There is so much good about America! Certainly, my expressions of concern in this volume should not be interpreted as disenchantment with our nation.

I am a product of public education, pre-school through doctoral study. I am also the product of a home in which the children learned early about God, and to love and honor Him. I have been influenced by the teachings of churches with which I have been associated through the years. Primarily because of my school, home, and church experiences, I have come to recognize that the <u>two greatest influences in shaping the lives of individuals and of</u>

nations are education (including the sciences) and religion, and that minimizing or eliminating either will deny achievement of the best of ourselves and of our nation.

Unfortunately, homes and churches, the traditional bastions of values education in America, have not in recent years reached young people to the extent they once did. In addition, the 20th century secularization of public schools in America has been a major factor in America's decline in its moral and spiritual values.

Our Founding Fathers wisely acknowledged, as noted in the First Amendment of our Constitution, that <u>Congress shall make no law respecting an establishment of religion</u>. The First Amendment also assures freedom of religious expression by each and every citizen.

Our nation was founded in the Judeo-Christian tradition. Interestingly, at the same time that our Founders were assuring freedom of religious expression for all of its citizens, they exercised their own newly-proclaimed freedom, and manifested their beliefs in God and in the teachings of the Old and New Testaments in the establishment of a great new democratic nation. We have always welcomed friends and neighbors of different faiths to the United States of America, assuring them that they are free to live and to practice fully their respective faiths, as long as they do not violate the laws of the land. That the United States of America was founded on Judeo-Christian values, however, is a historical fact.

Alexis De Tocqueville, a 19th century French statesman, historian, and social philosopher, traveled to America in the 1830s to discover the reasons for the success of this new nation. He was especially impressed with America's religious character, as indicated in the following statement, reported in *Toqueville's America— The Great Quotations*, edited by Frederick Kershner, Jr. (1).

> In France, I had almost always seen the spirit of religion and the spirit of freedom marching in opposite directions. But in America, I found that they were intimately united and that they reigned in

common over the same country (1), (pp. 62, 63).

What a magnificent heritage the United States of America has! What a solid base on which to establish the laws of our land! And, how good it is that those from other lands and religions are welcomed in a free America!

In order to continue to live, to enjoy, and to prosper in the United States of America, however, we who are now citizens (together with those from other nations and cultures who have become American citizens), must assume the heavy responsibilities essential to preserving the good life of our nation. Obviously, we have not always done such; and we are now in crisis, despite our affluence and our great technological and material gains.

This is a book that notes the decline in America's moral and spiritual values. It is written by someone who is a strong believer in, and an enthusiastic supporter of public education[a] and what it has accomplished in its teaching, research, and public service programs—someone who has served as a parent, grandparent, friend, counselor and/or teacher of countless numbers of young people for 65 years.

This is a book written to underscore for all Americans the seriousness of our present values' malaise. It acknowledges the harsh realities of America's decline in its moral and spiritual values, but also recognizes the inspiration and hope that can come with educational and spiritual forces working together to reverse our present values decline.

It is a call to homes and churches to once again assert their traditional leadership roles in providing values education to young people. It is a call to all agencies of society that influence the shaping of the lives of young people (including the various media, the courts, the entertainment industry, and the public schools, especially) to work together in alleviating our present values crisis. Special attention is given to the role of public schools in this volume because of their capability in reaching the masses of young people, and because of their ability to provide for academic learning and values learning concurrently.

This is a book in which the author speaks from a background of more than 82 years of diverse and abundant living, almost all of it in education—as a student, a teacher, a counselor, and an administrator. It is a book in which the author shares from his varied experiences locally, nationally, and internationally. It is a book in which he draws upon his spiritual commitment. Although neither a theologian nor a scholar in the field of religion, he calls on his personal faith and his varied educational experiences in discussing America's current decline in its values.

This book acknowledges the two greatest influences in shaping the lives of both individuals and nations: <u>education</u> and <u>religion</u>. In recent decades, however, we in America have given far more attention to the increasing of mankind's body of knowledge than we have to matters of spirit which are so essential to the proper management of how we use our abundant "know how." Without a spiritual rudder to direct the use of all we know—without the benefit of time-honored and time-proven values to guide us—we find ourselves as a people and as a nation, moving toward disaster, the way of other great nations in history that departed from their moral and spiritual moorings.

This is a book in which the author, having acknowledged the tremendous accomplishments of the intellect, calls for a corresponding level of attention to and understanding of the spiritual dimension in humankind's development! Such, in fact, is essential for our survival. Because of the current lag in attention to moral and spiritual considerations to guide us in the wise use of the great achievements of our minds, considerable attention is given to the dimension of <u>spirit</u> in *The Best of Mind and Spirit*, which makes this book by intent and to a substantial degree, a volume of <u>considerable spiritual emphasis</u>.

Finally, this book reflects the thinking of the author, and does not speak necessarily for others, or for institutions with which the author is now or has been associated. To be sure, there are references to other authors and their works that are relevant to *The Best of Mind and Spirit*. Deep appreciation is expressed to all that are quoted in this volume; and full credit is given to them both at the place of usage and again in the References that conclude *The Best of Mind and Spirit.*

Also, permission is hereby granted for readers to quote from what I have stated. The message of *The Best of Mind and Spirit* is one to be shared and, hopefully, will be helpful in dealing with America's current decline in its moral and spiritual values.

Guest Foreword

Educationally speaking, does mind exclude spirit? Whether science replaced moral philosophy, or research replaced teaching, gone is the emphasis on culture's grand religious narrative. What is left in our educational institutions? Yale law professor Stephen L. Carter finds a "culture of disbelief." According to him, scholars routinely ignore the spirit. Confronting the pluralistic academic dogmas of "established unbelief," historian George Marsden offers a Christian scholarship. Has this pattern of spiritual neglect always been there?

No! Scholars who chart historically the path of American public education instruct us by their many inclusions of knowledge and faith. From pre-revolution seminaries to large, multi-purpose Land-Grant and private institutions, people's religious beliefs definitely connected at the core of their educational institutions. One prominent Ivy League scholar supports a return of public religious affirmation.

Recently, Ronald F. Thiemann, Dean of Harvard Divinity School, lectured at Oklahoma State University. As for religion, he champions its expression in public affairs. Why should we emphasize moral and spiritual dimensions? According to public perceptions, social problems vary inversely with morality. Growing social problems—drugs, schoolyard shootings, Medicare fraud, family breakups, savings and loan scandals, increased sexual diseases—give society a knee jerk. So strong is the public's reaction that Nobel laureate Robert Foel says it's our "Fourth Great Awakening."

In *The Brothers Karamozov*, Dostoyevsky stated that "if God does not exist, everything is permissible." How can we account for our tolerant permissiveness? Are Americans abandoning their moral base? Are beliefs and ideals losing their hold? If the root cause of social decay comes from a moral and spiritual decline, aren't educational changes in order? This is why Robert B. Kamm has written *The Best of Mind and Spirit* as an educator's vision for the new millennium.

Through many years of living with and coming to love people throughout the world, Robert B. Kamm has witnessed firsthand how much religion enriches education. Since religion is largely neglected in public education, he calls for special efforts to strengthen the spiritual dimension. What we need, he believes, is a common vision for the common good. Could we, as Os Guiness and Ronald F. Thiemann suggest, develop a civil public square where people from any and all faiths can enter and freely share their beliefs?

Using the best of America's diverse citizenry, can educators publicly examine social problems? Yes, they can, for it's guaranteed by the Constitution. President Emeritus Kamm emphasizes the need for a "free marketplace" of religious expression on public education campuses and in public schools.

Professor Kamm sees two academic disciplines—one spiritual, the other mental—as being essential to the educating process. Taken together the process eventually equips students to secure their roles as responsible citizens. With this aim clearly in mind he proposes seven recommendations for education in general and five recommendations for teacher education in particular. Were these implemented, they would strengthen other efforts already underway. His suggestions are consistent with two popular educational trends—character education and the study of religion (world history). Why are these efforts popular? Such programs gain public support as they elevate character development and produce responsible citizens, especially in the face of the Paducah, Jonesboro, and Littleton school tragedies.

Through his educational vision for the 21st Century, he proposes a fusion of religious values into the mainstream of educating. Shouldn't we return to an emphasis on the best of mind and spirit? Can't we place greater trust in individuals who possess strong and honorable character? Clearly, the spiritual dimension can give people the positive motivation they need to do what is right and fair and just. Spiritual roots can also yield a crop of good stewards who discover meaning and purpose collectively.

As a sociologist I have studied "spiritual well-being" and noted certain benefits. People possessing this quality affirm life with God, value self worth and service to others. Other scholars report similar benefits: healthiness found in people's character, belief in society's rules and important cultural symbols. What exactly is "spiritual well-being?" Basically, it is synonymous with healthy self-concepts, faith, and belief in God, unselfish giving, living consistent with one's beliefs, personal satisfaction, moral character, and coping with life's uncertainties. Not surprisingly, such character qualities reside with those who hold strong religious beliefs.

Robert B. Kamm strives to be a consummate educator, one who honors God by his actions. His religious faith motivates exemplary conduct. Just as he left the Oklahoma State University presidency, Bill Bright founder of Campus Crusade for Christ said of him: "Of the university presidents I've met, Dr. Kamm stands out for his positive Christian witness and for advocating freedom of religious expression."

During his tenure as a teacher, dean, and president, he practiced an open door policy. He was available to students, some of whom approached the offices he held with anxiety. Once they met him, however, they saw him as a person of warmth. For him, faith is understood when expressed personally through actions. It is not only thinking but also being cordial that matters.

Achieving ambassador status, he served as the U.S. Delegate to the Executive Committee of the United Nations Educational, Scientific, and Cultural Organization; and he co-chaired the USA Delegation to the 1976 Nairobi World conference, interacting with educators, scientists and social leaders from 157 nations. Given the pluralism and global dimensions found in American society, who can best guide our thinking? We find in Professor Kamm a distinguished academician who speaks about what he knows and loves. His concern over our spiritual neglect prompted him to express his own Christian ideas. Now he asks those from other religions and religious faiths to join him and to bring the best of their beliefs to bear on our social problems.

As an arts and sciences dean, academic vice president, university president, and now president emeritus, he fully enjoys life. Educated in English, psychology, theater, and the humanities, he loves poetry, reads philosophy, respects scientific endeavors, and advocates freedom of religious expression. From my perspective, he exemplifies the best of mind and spirit because he models for students, faculty and staff, the very ideas he espouses. Throughout this book, he shares his vision of public education for this new millennium. His thinking provides a blueprint on how public educators and Americans generally can achieve freedom of, not freedom from, basic religious expressions. I applaud his efforts not just to analyze but also to address the underlying moral issues of our day.

—L. M. Hynson, Jr.
Stillwater, Oklahoma
January, 2001

Chapter I

An Overview

The United States of America, arguably the world's greatest nation, is experiencing a decline in its moral and spiritual values. One only has to read the newspapers and newsmagazines and to view television news and entertainment programs to realize this fact. As one who has observed and shared in the life of this richly blessed land of ours for many years, I (along with others) am deeply concerned with what is happening.

Through the years, I have come to recognize that <u>education and religion</u> are the two most powerful allies to our homes in shaping the lives of individuals and of nations. This is not to discount the high and essential roles and responsibilities of churches, the print media, the courts, and other agencies of society. It is simply to observe that <u>education and religion, working together</u>, hold the greatest promise to reverse the present values' decline.

When the word "education" is used we usually think of the formal, structured approach to education (with attention to both the sciences and the humanities), in which most USA[b] citizens participate for varying periods, pre-school through doctoral study. Along the way some depart and pursue other activities. The formal education experience continues for most people through secondary school, after which there is a reduction in numbers of those continuing in post-secondary study, with even smaller numbers continuing and completing advanced studies.

Some of life's most meaningful learning experiences, however, are those that come in our day-to-day activities. We become "educated" as the result of the totality of our experiences, inside class-rooms, in our homes and churches, by watching television, and in associating with others. The American poet, Walt Whitman, said it so well in, "There Was a Child Went Forth," in his book *Leaves of Grass* (2).

> There was a child went forth every day,
> And the first object he look'd upon, that object he
> became,
> And that object became part of him for the day or a
> certain part of the day,
> Or for many years or stretching cycles of years (2),
> (p. 305).

As we consider <u>education</u> and <u>religion</u> in this volume, I would note that there is not the same measure of understanding of religion as there is of education. In the pages that follow, <u>religion</u> will be used, for the most part, in a general sense. On other occasions, its usage may be more specific, in referring to one religious faith of the general grouping. (Chapter III provides a deeper and more thorough discussion of the subject.) At this point, I would add only that this volume is concerned with the highest and the best in spiritual expression and action.

Chapter II includes discussion of conditions, influences, and forces that have contributed to the present decline in the USA's moral and spiritual values. Among other considerations, it is evident that, in recent decades, increasing numbers of people have turned away from the moral and religious teachings of our spiritual leaders, as well as from the standards established by those who founded our nation. Some, in seeking for what is right and wrong, have come to rely on such "spur of the moment" changing values bases as, "Everybody is doing it, so it can't be too bad;" "If it works, it must be okay;" and, "If the situation demands it, do it." There is nothing predictable or stable in such man made, ever changing values' bases. We are operating increasingly without benefit of time-honored and time-proven "plumblines,"[c] such as the

Ten Commandments and the Golden Rule, which were basic in our nation's founding, and in shaping America's religious traditions and beliefs (as well as those of other nations of the world). Only as we look to the best in education and religion in the support of homes and families, can we hope to reverse present trends.

Chapter III underscores the need for <u>strong support in public education of homes and churches</u>, the essential lead institutions in values education. Before proceeding further, however, I wish to acknowledge the significant contributions of many privately supported education institutions in the shaping of our nation. I would note, in particular, the high role of church-founded educational institutions in initially providing quality education programs at all levels; and, especially, for what they have done (and many continue to do) in enhancing the moral and spiritual aspects of our lives. This volume deals largely with the role of public education that today serves the great masses of young people, and is called upon to assume even greater responsibility for moral and spiritual learning. It is recognized, at the same time, that some private education institutions today are not spiritually oriented, and the values education needs of their students may differ very little from those in public education institutions. It is hoped that what is discussed in this volume will be meaningful to all educational institutions and their students, faculty, and staff, be they publicly supported or privately endowed.

This volume acknowledges the wisdom of our Founders in stating in the First Amendment of our Constitution that <u>Congress shall make no law respecting an establishment of religion; and that all American citizens are free to worship as they choose</u>. In subsequent years, however, an erroneous interpretation by some that the First Amendment implies separation of Church and State has contributed substantially to the secularization of public education with the result that American public education has become virtually devoid of religious influence in recent decades. Such an interpretation was never intended by our Founders.

As we consider the roles of education and religion in serving today's masses of young people, we need to continue to affirm <u>the lead responsibilities and roles in values education of homes and churches</u>, especially in view of their lessened influence today. Public education efforts are needed in providing <u>continuing support</u> to those students who have received values education in their homes and/or churches, and especially for the great numbers of students who come with little or no home and/or church values orientation and emphasis. The job to be done is monumental—and, can be successful only if all agencies of society give wholehearted attention to today's values decline problem in America, including a <u>shared vision and understanding of what can be done through the combined efforts of all</u>.

Certainly, public education must not usurp or perform the traditional clerical roles of churches in serving the spiritual needs of their young people. But they can provide a free marketplace for all religious groups to fully manifest their beliefs, as well as encourage students to be active in the churches of their choice.

<u>Special attention to the academic dimension must also be given</u>, in view of the demands of the ever-changing and increasingly complex world in which we live. The quality of instruction, research, and service must continue to be enhanced, together with the proposed greater attention of public education to values education. Both can thrive in the academic setting.

America has no state church <u>by design</u>; and public education institutions may not provide a "pulpit" for any one religion. Each person may, however, speak freely of his or her faith—including the author of this volume. I share my thinking as a Christian, acknowledging always that <u>the same opportunity exists in the free marketplace of public education for all Americans of different faiths to speak freely and responsibly</u>.

This is a volume in which I recognize two highly meaningful national higher education associations in my professional life, together with some of their publications that have been helpful to me through the years. These are the National Association of State

Universities and Land-Grant Colleges (NASULGC); and the American Council on Education (ACE). Both are discussed in Chapter IV of this volume. Attention is given first to the Morrill Act of 1862 that provided for land-grant institutions, and to related developments in fulfilling the original act. Land-grant institutions were established to serve the sons and the daughters of the working classes in the areas of practical education, but not to the exclusion of the liberal arts. Also, from the beginning, emphasis was placed on students; and such continues, as evidenced by the fact that the first of five proposed reports by a recent NASULGC study group, the Kellogg Commission on the Future of State and Land-Grant Universities, is entitled *Returning to Our Roots: The Student Experience* (3). Subsequent reports deal with "access," "engaged institutions," "a learning society," and "campus culture."

Also, in Chapter IV is discussion of the second of the two aforementioned higher education associations that have meant so much to me, the American Council on Education, together with two of its publications. Early in my professional career I became acquainted with the ACE's *The Personnel Point of View* (rev. ed.) (4) which first appeared in 1937, and was published in 1949. In it, the concept of education was broadened to include attention to the student's well-rounded development—physically, socially, emotionally, and spiritually, as well as academically.

A second significant ACE publication that is also relevant to the discussions of this volume is the ACE Summer/Fall 1997 issue of the *Educational Record* (5). It is devoted entirely to "College and Character: Preparing Students for Lives of Civic Responsibility," discussed more fully in Chapter IV.

As we consider a proposed shared role of education and religion in coping with the current decline in our nation's values, we need also to take note that ours is a pluralistic society, with increasingly more and different faiths represented in the student bodies and on the faculties of our public schools, colleges, and universities. As part of my education through the years, I have been privileged to have considerable international involvement, which is discussed in more detail in Chapter V.

Chapter VI presents "from where I come" as the result of my educational and religious backgrounds. I have been fortunate in that I was able to correlate these experiences early in life and subsequently to enjoy a long and rewarding career in public education.

Chapters VII, VIII, and IX build on the previous six chapters of *The Best of Mind and Spirit* in the offering of some specific proposals of steps to be taken, which can be helpful in dealing with our nation's decline in its moral and spiritual values. Attention is given in Chapter VII to the essential need for strong leadership in public education today to bring to fruition the proposed emphases on concurrent academic and religious learning and to manage the host of other issues, needs, and responsibilities confronting educators today. This level of leadership will assure excellence in teaching, research, outreach, and public service (including the securing of necessary funding).

Reference has been made to the free marketplace for religious expression in America—including public education—as guaranteed by the Constitution of the USA. A number of proposals of what may be done in public education institutions in support of religious awareness and development, concurrent with academic growth, are presented. I would underscore that <u>whatever is done should be done by educators themselves</u>—teachers, counselors, administrators, and other staff personnel in concert with those in homes and churches. Such <u>should not be mandated by government officials, or by non-educators</u>.

Chapter VIII concentrates on the day-to-day roles of teachers, counselors, mentors, coaches, and others who work especially closely with students to assure them the opportunities and freedoms that are theirs and to provide proper emphasis on both academic and religious learning. Recognizing that a turn-around of America's current decline in its moral and spiritual values may take years, the final pages of Chapter VIII deal with the need to provide a program especially designed to orient teachers-in-training to their roles and responsibilities in subsequent years so they may acquaint their students with the values crisis in America and what may and can be done to alleviate the situation.

Primary attention in Chapters VII and VIII is given to the role of public education in dealing with our values crisis, Chapter IX underscores the need for concurrent, meaningful involvement of other agencies of society—homes, churches, the courts, the media, and the entertainment industry.

In many ways, Chapter II and Chapter IX are companion chapters. In originally presenting and discussing some problem areas in Chapter II, certain references are made that contain both discussion of problem areas and proposals of what may be done to alleviate the problems. In Chapter IX, little supplementary attention is given to what was presented earlier in Chapter II. Chapter IX does, however, repeat some statements deliberately for purposes of emphasis and/or continuity.

There then follows an Epilogue that sums up the spirit and the message of *The Best of Mind and Spirit*. The Appendices present several of the author's addresses and publications through the years that are relevant and supportive of the present volume.

One cannot deal with a subject of the magnitude of *The Best of Mind and Spirit* without referring to the experiences and wisdom of others. A section entitled References lists names or sources that have benefited the author. The format is one of providing references with identifying numbers, 1-154. Also, a listing of Biblical References and statements of endorsement are provided.

I am deeply grateful for all that have contributed to *The Best of Mind and Spirit* through their spoken or written words. When quotations of others are used, acknowledgement of authorship and publication(s) containing the quotations are indicated.

Also, I would note that, in addition to the above statement, there are (at the beginning, and at the end of *The Best of Mind and Spirit*) expressions of appreciation and the granting of full credit to authors and to their respective publishers.

Chapter II

The Moral and Spiritual Decline in America

Before discussing what I regard to be America's number one problem, I would acknowledge, once again, that ours continues to be the greatest nation in the world! So many times those from other lands have spoken to me of their high regard for America's way of life, which they desire for themselves and their families. I like the following words about America and its opportunities as expressed in Thomas Wolfe's book entitled *You Can't Go Home Again* (6). He observed:

> So then to every man his chance—to every man, regardless of his birth, his shining, golden opportunity—to every man the right to live, to work, to be himself, and to become whatever his manhood and his vision can combine to make him—this, seeker, is the promise of America (6), (p. 393).

Although from an earlier time in America's history, these words continue to have meaning for us today. In fact, as a first generation American, I am deeply indebted and grateful to the America into which I was privileged to be born!

The people of America of all ages are <u>good</u> people, for the most part. In addition to our material goods, we give generously of ourselves—even our lives in helping those in need throughout the world. We are known as a nation of volunteers in assisting others. And yet, we've lost ground in recent decades in the eyes of many abroad, as well as among our own citizenry.

Perhaps the most insidious factor in America's values decline is that many <u>good</u> Americans do not take seriously the reality of this problem. Many of us are concerned, but we either do not know what to do, or elect not to get involved in reversing the present deadly trend. And there are other areas, by omission or commission, which have contributed to our present decline in values including secularized public schools, some of the media, and the entertainment industry, to mention a few.

There are those who shrug off such observations, pointing out, "There have always been problems in our nation, so why worry?" Others note, "We've never had it so good," which is true in some ways. In the net, however, America is in trouble so far as its values are concerned. There is need to face that reality and to do so "the sooner, the better" if this richly blessed nation of ours is to survive as the world's greatest and most cherished nation.

In the pages that follow, I wish to concentrate primarily on efforts to understand and to deal with what is happening in our great land.

IMPRIMIS (taking its name from the Latin term "in the first place") is the publication of Hillsdale College, located at Hillsdale, Michigan. In its May, 1998 issue was an article by John Fund, a member of the Editorial Board of the *Wall Street Journal*, entitled "Politics, Economics, and Education in the 21st Century" (7).[d] He noted the gravity of the problem and (encouragingly) also observed that people are telling pollsters:

> The single greatest threat to future generations is the decline of morals and ethical standards. Fortunately, these individuals aren't content merely to voice their fears; they are doing something about them. In other words, they are leading a moral counterrevolution. They are buying millions of copies of values oriented texts like William Bennett's *Book of Virtues*. They are founding thousands of home

10

school cooperatives and hundreds of new private schools. They are joining dozens of traditionalist groups like Promise Keepers, Focus on the Family, and the Christian Coalition. And in towns and cities across the land, they are rebuilding the "little platoons" of family, church, and community that are the basis of the free society.

Robert H. Bork, nominated by former USA President Ronald Reagan to serve as a member of the United States Supreme Court (but not confirmed by the United States Senate), has written a book entitled *Slouching Towards Gomorrah* (8). I quote from the Introduction of his book:

Large chunks of the moral life of the United States, major features of its culture, have disappeared altogether, and more are in process of extinction. These are being, or have already been replaced by new modes of conduct, ways of thought, and standards of morality that are unwelcome to many of us (8).

As mentioned earlier, we read and hear much about today's "new morality," "situational ethics," and "postmodernism." Having departed from such absolutes as the Ten Commandments and the Golden Rule, many of our citizens are guided by thoughts like these: "If it works, it must be right;" "If the situation demands it, do it;" "If it feels good, do it;" and "Everyone is doing it, so it must be OK." We are confused about what is right or wrong, good or evil! We are living in times when, in the name of freedom, anything goes—obscenities, foul language, cheating on our marriage partners, and disrespect for law and that which is uplifting and good.

On occasion, our courts may have gone too far in permitting (in the name of freedom) some behavior that is not in the best interests of the majority of our citizens. Actually, freedom is not license to say and to do whatever we wish! Rather, freedom permits us to say and to do <u>the responsible thing</u>—to act within the law, and to say and to do that which is good and noble, and which makes for a better society.

In my readings and research for *The Best of Mind and Spirit*, I have encountered a few members of the press who do not understand freedom as just defined; but I have found also that the vast majority of members of the press are highly responsible. I have been privileged to call upon those who write for newspapers, newsmagazines, professional journal reports, professional association releases, the Associated Press, and the United Press. In the writing of my book, I have depended considerably on the reports of the press, and I am most appreciative and grateful to them.

In the July, 1997 issue of *U.S. News and World Report* (9), John Leo commented on "A No-Fault Holocaust." He noted the following:

> In 20 years of college teaching, Prof. Robert Simon has never met a student who denied that the Holocaust happened. What he sees quite often, though, is worse: students who acknowledge the fact of the Holocaust but can't bring themselves to say that killing millions of people is wrong. Simon reports that 10 to 20 percent of his students think this way. Usually they deplore what the Nazis did, but their disapproval is expressed as a matter of taste or personal preference, not moral judgment. "Of course I dislike the Nazis," one student told Simon, "but who is to say they are morally wrong?"

In a lead editorial in the November 16, 1998 issue of *Christianity Today*, entitled "Poster Boy for Postmodernism" (10), Charles Colson and Nancy Pearcey, observed:

> As we write, there is a growing clamor for President Clinton to leave the Oval Office; but across the country there is a clamor to throw someone else out—in this case, David Cash, a student at the

University of California at Berkeley. The latter case, though hardly drawing the same attention, may nonetheless have even graver implications for our nation's future.

The controversy over Cash arises from a gruesome case last year in which a California teenager, Jeremy Strohmeyer, sexually molested and murdered a seven-year-old girl in a Las Vegas casino. Cash witnessed what his friend was doing but did not stop him and later agreed to keep quiet.

The authors noted that "the core of postmodernism is a rejection of universal truth claims and moral principles." Additionally, they observed that "the bill on postmodernism is coming due. Either we will pay its bloody price, or find our way back to the truths that make civilization possible."

Part of our current confusion about right and wrong can be attributed to the fact that, as mentioned earlier, the thoughts and positions of many so-called "good people"—those who do discern between right and wrong—are not being expressed. There is a reluctance, and sadly, a lack of courage on the parts of many to "stand up and be counted." For them, it is easier to turn their backs to the realities of evil and wait for the wrongs to correct themselves—something that, in all probability, will never happen. And all the while these good folks wait, many becoming callused to the continued existence of the very evils they once deplored. They soon find they are no longer sensitive to the wrongs, and they join the crowds, taking comfort in their material gains, their newfound acceptance in certain circles, the "fun" they're having, and the new gods they've created for themselves!

We must not minimize the negative impact of America's "new morality" and of postmodernism on young people today. To abandon the universal truths and the moral and spiritual teachings that have guided civilizations in the past will surely lead to the downfall of our own beloved nation.

Later in this volume we will continue this discussion, noting that only with a return to a recognition that we are God's—that our bodies, our minds, our total beings are God's—will we be able to put all things into proper perspective.

As I write I am aware of much that is wrong—much, in fact, that many of us no longer recognize as wrong! At the same time, I must, in all fairness, acknowledge the commendable efforts of those who continue the fight against that which is wrong. I have referred earlier to the decline of home and family influence, but it would be unfair to overlook the fact that many homes (including single-parent homes) continue to reach young people and to serve them well in providing moral and spiritual guidance.

There has been a reduction of home and family influence in the development of values of many of today's young people. With so many working mothers and the large number of single-parent homes without shared parenting efforts of mother and father, unsupervised television viewing often serves as "baby-sitter" and various out-of-home activities are beyond the control of parents.

In a volume entitled *Choose Life* (11), authored by Rabbi Bernard Mandelbaum,[e] John Stuart Mill (12), an English philosopher and economist, is quoted as follows:

> Moral and religious education consist in training the feelings and daily habits ... It is the home, the family, which gives us the moral or religious education we really receive (12), (p. 71).

In the sixth chapter of Deuteronomy in the Old Testament of the Bible are the following words spoken by Moses:

> Hear, O Israel: The Lord our god is one Lord: And thou shalt love the Lord thy God with all thine heart, and with all thy soul, and with all thy might. And these words, which I command thee this day, shall be in thine heart: And thou shalt teach them diligently unto thy children, and shalt talk of them when thou sittest in thine house, and when thou

walkest by the way, and when thou liest down, and when thou risest up. And thou shalt bind them for a sign upon thine hand, and they shall be as frontlets between thine eyes. And thou shalt write them upon the posts of thy house, and on thy gates (Deuteronomy 6:4-9).

Additional discussion about the lead role of home and family in moral training, together with suggestions for what may be done to develop it, is presented in Chapter IX.

In some of our churches, as in many of our homes, there has been a lessening of an earlier strong involvement in emphasizing moral and spiritual values development of young people. This trend can be attributed, in part, to the failure of parents to provide religious teachings in the home and to take their young people to church and to church school. This sends a wrong message to their offspring that spiritual development and participation in church activities really are not very important.

Churches, through their outreach and "ministry beyond walls," do, however, continue to attract the young, whether churched or previously unchurched. Among them are those that are strongly Bible-oriented. Additionally, such ministries as Campus Crusade for Christ, The American Bible Society, and Navigators speak to the preferences of young people today. The facts are that many continue to be in need of the best efforts of churches and other ministries, as mentioned above.

Ralph Cooley has served with the Campus Ministry at the University of Idaho since 1977. In the September/October, 1997 issue of *Worldwide Challenge* (13), a publication of Campus Crusade for Christ, he reported how students have changed in their religious knowledge and beliefs during his two decades as a campus minister. He noted:

When I first started ministry here, about 98 percent of the students believed in God, and the majority had some type of church background, so there was a

15

foundation that we could build on. Over the course of 20 years, the statistics have changed. Still about 90 percent believe in a god, but that view of God has radically changed; it ranges anywhere from a biblical view to Eastern mysticism to whatever god you want to make up. A large majority of students now come from unchurched families with no knowledge of Christ or the Bible.

In the Summer/Fall issue of *Educational Record* (5), William H. Willimon, dean of the Chapel and professor of Christian ministry at Duke University, wrote about "Religious Faith and Development of Character on Campus" (14).[f] Additional attention is given to Willimon's article in subsequent chapters, but I would note at this point, that (relevant to the present discussion), Willimon makes reference to a book authored by George Marsden, entitled *The Soul of the American University: From Protestant Establishment to Established Nonbelief* (15).

As we attempt to understand reasons for our nation's decline in moral and spiritual values, I, as an educator, must admit that our public education institutions share in the responsibility for values decline. This is not so much a result of what we have done directly as of education's failure to deal with certain forces—including the secularization of education—that have altered its course in the past half century. At the same time that I acknowledge the above, I also would note once again that public education institutions are our best hope to reverse the present values decline. Actually, central to the mission of this volume are suggestions of how public education institutions, in cooperative and supportive roles with homes and churches, can help to get America back on track, morally and spiritually. As mentioned earlier, only our public education institutions have the capability to reach the masses of America's young people today. We in public education can and must assume a more active role in support of and collaboration with homes and churches (as well as with other concerned agencies of society) in bringing the best of mind and spirit together.

16

How can public education assist in resolving the problem, if as just suggested it is partly responsible for the present values crisis? I believe the time has come—in fact, is overdue—to undo the secularization of public education. We must take a strong stand against the current highly questionable interpretation of the intent of the authors of the First Amendment of the Constitution. I support fully the First Amendment that clearly states that "Congress shall make no law respecting an establishment of religion, or prohibiting the free exercise thereof." I do not support the concept of "separation of church and state" which has no constitutional basis.

The emphasis of this volume, which has already been stated and will be mentioned repeatedly, is on <u>the best of both mind and spirit</u>. The best of both is achievable when education and religion join forces once again.

In my own lifetime, I have seen framed copies of the Ten Commandments in public schoolrooms along with pictures of the Founders of America and their words of wisdom. Religious holidays (including the Fourth of July, originally celebrated as a religious holiday) were respected in the past. Time was taken for Religious Emphasis Days in public schools, colleges, and universities with speakers <u>representing the</u> different <u>faith groups of the student body</u> participating. Until well into the 20th Century there was in American schools ready acknowledgment of God as Lord and as Creator as emphasized by our Founders.

To be sure, the situation was less complex in earlier years than in today's increasingly pluralistic society. However, instead of finding a solution that respects the diverse faiths of students and encourages them in the free expression of their respective faiths, we have elected to support a position of limiting the role of religion in the public education process.

Kenneth Irving Brown, former president of Hiram College and Denison University, wrote a significant volume in 1954 entitled *Not Minds Alone* (16). Speaking as a Christian higher education president, and directed primarily to those serving in Christian higher education, he noted:

> ... we have gone to perilous extremes and separat-
> ed education from religion in ways our forefathers
> and their children never intended (16), (p. 16).

What a tragedy that many millions of American young people have been limited in their values education, while progressing with their academic learnings! The situation for those who have been denied values education and who subsequently become parents is that they <u>are unable or unwilling to teach their own children about spiritual matters and to encourage their offspring to participate in church and religious activities.</u>

I sense a very real kinship with Dr. Brown. I have a deep appreciation for what is said in his book *Not Minds Alone*, sub-titled *Some Frontiers of Christian Education*. Published in 1954, it has been a very meaningful volume to me. Now, some 47 years later, as a public educator, I seek to enhance the spiritual dimension as part of the total educational experience of <u>all students</u> today, with special attention to the masses of young people of many different religious faiths, pre-school through doctoral study. I believe that such is possible within the framework of the wise stipulations of the First Amendment of our Constitution.

There are steps that can be taken by public education to open doors for the moral and spiritual development of young people who may have been denied such in recent decades because of the secularization of public education in America. I sense a readiness on the part of many students for greater attention to matters of the spirit. Some suggestions of what may be done are presented in Chapter IX, but for the moment let us give further thought to some problems before us.

Certainly, the creation-evolution issue deserves some attention as we view the current decline in America's moral and spiritual values.

Acknowledging that there are differences between those committed to a spiritual position relating to creation and those who support evolution, I would note that there are many scientists of deep spiritual faith; and there are many people of deep spiritual faith who are scientists. A distinguished colleague of mine at Oklahoma State University for more than 40 years has been Dr. Duane Peterson, Professor and Head of the Veterinary Medicine Anatomy Department, 1948-1972, and Regents Professor, 1973-1986 (17). He received the College of Veterinary Medicine's "Teacher of the Year" award in 1961, 1964, 1969, and 1971, as well as the "Teacher of the Year" award for the entire university in 1971.

In an address on the Oklahoma State University campus April 8, 1998, he stated:

> I believe God is a living God and is still creating; He expects man to comport and live up to God's reason for creating him.

Additionally, he observed:

> Genesis 1 states in verses 27 and 28, "So God created man in his own image, in the image of God created He him; male and female created He them. And God blessed them, and God said unto them, 'Be fruitful, and multiply and replenish the earth,' (He did not say to overpopulate it;) 'and subdue it; and have dominion over the fish of the sea, and over the fowl of the air, and over every living thing that moveth upon the earth.'"

> It would seem that God needed the expertise of a CEO and thus allowed certain leaders to effect the responsibility of the management of His kingdom. To this end God endowed the genus Homo (meaning man) and the species sapiens (meaning wise or sageness). To effect this He created special anatomical and physiological features in man.

> He gave man a very large brain to think and reason

and hopefully to make rational judgments. He also gave man a specialized larynx to vocalize and communicate to a much greater extent than any of the other higher animals. In addition He created a unique estrous cycle by which man might be in control of the human population. He also gave man apposability or the ability for the thumb to touch all of the other digits (fingers), allowing man to develop skills to operate digital and computer equipment that are so much a part of today's society.

Dr. Peterson concluded his statement by adding:

Man has not met God's expectations. Man has advanced in his mental, scientific, digital and computer skills but his moral behavior patterns have declined. His sexual patterns have become more animalistic and show a lack of personal responsibility. The latter two traits have defied God's Ten Commandments. They also have defied the use of the special creative features which God gave to man as listed in the previous paragraph.

In another presentation on the Oklahoma State University campus, April 14, 1999, Dr. Sam Fuhlendorf, a member of the faculty of the Department of Plant and Soil Science (18), spoke of "The Dichotomy of Evolution." In his introductory comments, he observed:

Evolution is a topic that has been controversial to Christians since its introduction into the scientific community. Much of the controversy has developed through discussions from the secular and Christian media and has led to misunderstandings between scientists and Christians. This controversy has resulted in a dichotomy of terminology and focus that limit the ability of each group to effectively communicate to the other.

Over the past several years, it has become apparent to me that many Christians vociferously opposed to evolution are not aware of the scientific community's approach to evolution. Christians have largely focused on attempts to apply evolution to the origins of man, while the majority of the scientific community is interested in the mechanisms of genetic change of organisms as they adapt to environmental change. It is my intention to present my perspective on this issue and introduce the topic of evolution as it is taught and discussed within scientific circles. As a scientist and a Christian, it is important to me that my fellow Christians understand that the topic of evolution is much broader than the origins of humans and that accusations directed toward evolutionary scientists are often unfounded and may be counterproductive.

Additionally, I share a quotation of a third colleague at Oklahoma State University, Dr. James Breazile, Professor of Physiology in the College of Veterinary Medicine (19). He holds D.V.M. and Ph.D. degrees, as well as a Masters degree in theology. He is an ordained deacon in the Catholic Church. In a recent visit with him he observed:

Recognizing that different truths may be derived from widely varying sources, I believe that truth can never contradict truth. It seems impossible for the person who seeks and finds scientific truth, and applies rational thought to it, to deny that a higher truth lies behind his discovery. It is not possible therefore, for a well-trained and serious scientist to fail to recognize the existence of God.

And, Dr. Kyle Yates, long-time holder of the Phoebe Schertz

21

Young Chair in Religious Studies and the head emeritus of the department of Religion at Oklahoma State University (20), has observed:

> Because of a combined degree in natural sciences and teaching experience in anthropology, archaeology and world religions, I have watched the ebb and flow of conflict between science and religion with ever increasing interest. Often this conflict approached the status of war. More often than not, the conflict arose out of misunderstanding or mistaken zeal by both camps. Since knowledge and truth are approached from almost opposite perspectives, the element of conflict is built in.
>
> Extremes have produced either "divine" intolerance or "secular" arrogance. This is not necessary! I discovered that my scientific methods in archaeological field excavations did not conflict with my concern about matters of faith or history. On the contrary, each strengthened the other when properly understood. The real impasse occurs when one group (science or religion) denies any legitimate place in the contemporary world for the other. Science has dominated much of American life, especially in the field of education, invariably pushing religion to the sidelines. However, religionists have tended to push back equally hard, sometimes to their own detriment.
>
> Total truth is neither the property of religion nor science. Each has much to offer in overall contribution to society. It is time to bury both the daggers and the diatribes.

At this point, as we consider the various issues and problems relevant to America's present decline in its moral and spiritual values, we would do well to remind ourselves that in our nation's beginning we were founded on moral and spiritual bases. To assure that we stay focused and on track, let us look at the facts of our founding (so far as religious beliefs and practices are concerned), as reported in *One Nation Under God* (21), prepared by the Christian Defense Fund, Benjamin Hart, President.[9]

John Adams, the USA's second president (after serving as George Washington's vice president, and as a member of the Continental Congress) wrote the following in his diary on February 22, 1756 (22):

> Suppose a nation in some distant region should take the Bible for their only law book, and every member should regulate his conduct by the precepts there exhibited! Every member would be obliged in conscience to temperance, frugality, and industry; to justice, kindness, and charity towards his fellowmen; and to piety, love, and reverence toward Almighty God.... What a Utopia, what a Paradise would this region be (21), (p. 5).

On July 3, 1776, John Adams made this statement regarding America's decision the previous day to declare independence from Great Britain (23):

> The second day of July, 1776, will be the most memorable epoch in the history of America, to be celebrated by succeeding generations as the great anniversary festival, commemorated as the day of deliverance by solemn acts of devotion to God Almighty from one end of the Continent to the other, from this time forward forevermore (21), (p. 6).

Samuel Adams, a cousin of John Adams and known as "Father of the American Revolution," asserted in his 1772 document, "The Rights of the Colonists," the following (24):

The right to freedom being the gift of the Almighty ... The rights of the colonists as Christians ... may be best understood by reading and carefully studying the institutions of The Great Law Giver and Head of the Christian Church, which are to be found clearly written and promulgated in the New Testament (21), (p. 7).

As the Declaration of Independence was being signed in 1776, Samuel Adams declared (25):

We have this day restored the Sovereign to Whom all men ought to be obedient. He reigns in Heaven and from the rising to the setting of the sun, let His kingdom come (21), (p. 7, 8).

Also, in his Last Will and Testament Samuel Adams wrote (26):

Principally, and first of all, I resign my soul to the Almighty Being who gave it, and my body I commit to the dust, relying on the merits of Jesus Christ for the pardon of my sins (21), (p. 8).

On September 6, 1774, (27), the Continental Congress made its first official act a call for prayer; on September 11, 1777, (27), the Continental Congress ordered the importation of 20,000 Bibles for the American troops; and on October 18, 1780 (27), the Continental Congress issued another proclamation for a Day of Public Thanksgiving and Prayer—all as reported in *One Nation Under God* (21), (pp. 8, 9, 10).

On July 13, 1787, the Continental Congress passed "An Ordinance for the Government of the Territory of the United States" (28), as reported in *One Nation Under God* (21), (p. 11). This law was passed again by the United States Congress and signed into law by President George Washington on August 4, 1789 (28), as also reported in *One Nation Under God* (21), (p. 11).

Article III stated:

Religion, morality, and knowledge being necessary to

good government and the happiness of mankind, schools and the means of education shall be forever encouraged (21), (p. 11).

When the War of Independence drew to a close, the Continental Congress became the Congress of the United States of America (21), (p. 12). Both the House of Representatives and the Senate named Chaplains (21), (p. 12); and the practice continues today.

On September 25, 1789, (28), Congress unanimously approved a resolution asking President George Washington to proclaim a National Day of Thanksgiving, as follows:

> Day of Thanksgiving. Resolved. That a joint committee of both Houses be directed to wait upon the President of the United States to request that he recommend to the people of the United States a day of public thanksgiving and prayer, to be observed by acknowledging, with grateful hearts, the many signal favors of Almighty God, especially by affording them an opportunity peaceably to establish a constitution of government for their safety and happiness (21), (pp. 12, 13).

Subsequent to the request from Congress, on October 3, 1789, from the City of New York, President Washington proclaimed a National Day of Thanksgiving, and there has followed, through the years, annual proclamations by USA presidents for a Day of Thanksgiving (21), (p. 66).

Following is Abraham Lincoln's frequently quoted proclamation of October 3, 1863, 74 years later, as shared in *Collected Works of Abraham Lincoln*, Basler, Roy P., Editor (29).

> The year that is drawing towards its close has been filled with the blessings of fruitful fields and healthful skies. To these bounties, which are so constantly enjoyed that we are prone to forget the source from

which they come, others have been added, which are of so extraordinary a nature, that they cannot fail to penetrate and soften even the heart which is habitually insensible to the ever watchful providence of Almighty God.... No human counsel hath devised nor hath any mortal hand worked out (America's great blessings). They are the gracious gifts of the Most High God, who, while dealing with us in anger for our sins, hath nevertheless remembered mercy. It has seemed to me fit and proper that they should be solemnly, reverently and gratefully acknowledged as with one heart and one voice by the whole American People. I do therefore invite my fellow citizens in every part of the United States, . . . to set apart and observe the last Thursday of November next, as a day of Thanksgiving and Praise to our beneficent Father who dwelleth in the heavens. And I recommend to them that while offering up the ascriptions justly due to Him for such singular deliverances and blessings, they do also, with humble penitence for our national perverseness and disobedience, . . . fervently implore the interposition of the Almighty Hand to heal the wounds of the nation and to restore it as soon as may be consistent with the Divine purposes to the full enjoyment of peace, harmony, tranquillity and Union (29), (pp. 496, 497).

Additional quotations from *One Nation Under God* (21) prepared by the Christian Defense Fund follow. On July 4, 1776, the delegates to the Continental Congress formally declared our independence from Great Britain (30), (p. 13). Following are the words of the Declaration of Independence:

When in the Course of human events, it becomes necessary for one people to dissolve the political bands which have connected them with another, and to assume among the powers of the earth the separate and equal station to which the Laws of Nature and of Nature's God entitles them. . . .

We hold these truths to be self-evident, that all men are created equal. That they are endowed by their Creator with certain unalienable rights, that among these are life, liberty and the pursuit of happiness. . . .

We, Therefore, the Representatives of the United States of America, in General Congress, Assembled, appealing to the Supreme Judge of the world for the rectitude of our intentions. . . .

And for the support of this Declaration, with a firm reliance on the protection of Divine Providence, we mutually pledge to each other our lives, our fortunes, and our sacred honor (21), (pp. 13, 14).

Benjamin Franklin was one of America's most influential and famous Founding Fathers (31). In his Autobiography he wrote:

I have been religiously educated as a Presbyterian; and ... I was never without religious principles (21), (p. 19).

I never doubted, for instance, the existence of the Deity; that He made the world, and governed it by His Providence; that the most acceptable service of God was the doing good to man; that our souls are immortal; and that all crime will be punished, and virtue rewarded, either here or hereafter (21), (p. 19).

In a letter of March 1778, to the Ministry of France (32), he wrote:

A Bible and a newspaper in every house, a good school in every district—all studied and appreciated as they merit—are the principal support of virtue, morality, and civil liberty (21), (p. 21).

On June 28, 1787, the Constitutional Convention was deadlocked and embroiled in bitter controversy (33). Benjamin Franklin rose and made the following plea to the delegates:

> I have lived, Sir, a long time, and the longer I live, the more convincing proofs I see of this truth—that God governs in the affairs of men. And if a sparrow cannot fall to the ground without His notice, is it probable that an empire can rise without His aid?
>
> We have been assured, Sir, in the Sacred Writings, that "except the Lord build the House, they labor in vain that build it." I firmly believe this; and I also believe that without His concurring aid we shall succeed in this political building no better than the builders of Babel: We should be divided by our partial local interests; our projects will be confounded, and we ourselves shall become a reproach and bye word down to future ages. . . .
>
> I therefore beg leave to move—that henceforth prayers imploring the assistance of Heaven, and its blessing on our deliberations, be held in this Assembly every morning before we proceed to business, and that one or more of the clergy of this city be requested to officiate in that service (21), (pp. 23, 24).

Alexander Hamilton, a signer of the Constitution and one of America's most preeminent Founding Fathers, was author of 51 of the 85 Federalist papers, which powerfully made the case for ratifying the Constitution (34). He was Secretary of the Treasury in George Washington's administration (21), (p. 24). Shortly after the Constitutional Convention of 1787 (34), Hamilton stated:

> For my own part, I sincerely esteem it a system

which without the finger of God, never could have been suggested and agreed upon by such a diversity of interests (21), (p. 24).

A famous Revolutionary leader and orator, Patrick Henry said, "Give me liberty, or give me death," which became the battle cry of the American Revolution (35). He was a five-time Governor of Virginia. He once declared:

It cannot be emphasized too strongly or too often that this great nation was founded, not by religion-ists, but by Christians; not on religions, but on the Gospel of Jesus Christ. For this very reason peoples of other faiths have been afforded asylum, prosper-ity, and freedom of worship here (21), (p. 26).

On another occasion he said, pointing to his Bible (36):

The Bible is worth all other books which have ever been printed (21), (pp. 26, 27).

James Madison, known as the father of the U.S. Constitution, was the primary author of the Bill of Rights and engineered the Louisiana Purchase of 1803. He was also the fourth President of the United States. Madison believed Christianity to be the foun-dation upon which a just government must be built. Writing on June 20, 1785 (37), he stated:

Religion [is] the basis and Foundation of Govern-ment (21), (p. 41).

Madison expounded further (38):

We have staked the whole future of American civi-lization, not upon the power of government, far from it. We have staked the future of all of our political institutions upon the capacity of mankind for self-government; upon the capacity of each and all of us to govern ourselves, to control ourselves, to sustain ourselves according to the Ten Commandments of God (21), (pp. 41, 42).

In 1788, Madison stated (39):

> The belief in God all powerful, wise, and good, is so
> essential to the moral order of the world and to the
> happiness of man, that arguments which enforce it
> cannot be drawn from too many sources nor adapt-
> ed with too much solicitude to the different charac-
> ters and capacities to be impressed with it (21), (p.
> 42).

Other expressions of religious beliefs of our nation's leaders
could be mentioned. I would share but one more at this time.
Some 80 years later in our nation's history, on September 5, 1864,
the Committee of Colored People from Baltimore presented
President Lincoln with a Bible (40). Here is what Lincoln told
them in his speech:

> In regard to this Great Book, I have but to say, I
> believe the Bible is the best gift God has given to
> man. All the good Savior gave to the world was com-
> municated through this Book. But for this Book we
> could not know right from wrong. All things most
> desirable for man's welfare, here and hereafter, are
> to be found portrayed in it. To you I return my most
> sincere thanks for the elegant copy of the great
> Book of God which you present (21), (pp. 40, 41).

There are some people today who think there is need to
rewrite the Constitution of the United States of America—that
our Founding Fathers wrote a document that is no longer relevant.
To be sure, through the years, there have been occasional changes
made in the Constitution for purposes of clarification, but nothing of a substantial nature to change this magnificent document
has been accomplished.

What a frightening prospect, however, is the possibility of
altering our nation's Constitution! To an extent, the present

decline in our nation's moral and spiritual values suggests that there may have been some departures from the wisdom and intent of those who founded our nation. Fortunately, however, we continue to be guided by the words of the Constitution of the USA, essentially as originally written. And yet, the very fact that there are those today that argue for a new, modern version of our Constitution suggests how serious our current problems may be.

Through the years, we as a nation have been blessed with sound leadership in times of great crisis. Our own Civil War in the 19th Century and communism in its efforts to take over the world in the 20th Century are examples.

In many ways, our nation's present values crisis, with the secularization of American public education (as well as of other segments of our society), presents us with problems in our own land that are more immediately upon us and more threatening to the continuation of the greatness of America than is communism which has been, and continues to be, fought primarily on foreign soil. The overriding common element in both the takeover by communism of many nations in earlier years and in America's present values crisis has been a turning away from God by many. It was, however, America's traditionally strong spiritual resources and vast technological capabilities that led to a substantial reduction of the influence of communism in the world. And it will take the best of mind and spirit—the best of education and of religion working together—to reverse the present crisis of America's decline in its moral and spiritual values.

I would observe at this point that there is much confusion today about the meaning and the practice of freedom. Some of us confuse freedom with license to do whatever we wish. In certain situations, we say and do whatever we desire. We tend to overlook the fact that in a free society freedom is built on responsibility. We are free within law to say and to do that which is responsible and serves the common good. Yes, we are guaranteed freedom of speech by the First Amendment of our Constitution, but that does not give us the right to engage in immoral speech, to print obscene materials, or to include offensive behavior in radio, movies, television, or Internet presentations.

Part of our current problem is that some of our courts have tended to favor individuals who cry censorship when questions are raised about what they say or do. We are experiencing a time when the wishes of individuals (regardless of how questionable their words or actions may be) are supported, in some cases, above the wishes of offended groups. If there are efforts to curb certain expressions or activities in the print media, on television, in the movies, or on the Internet, objections are raised by those responsible for the questionable activities. They frequently overlook the fact that censorship of offensive materials, speech, and actions existed in America centuries before the recent emergence of the "new morality."

Our homes and families, our schools, our libraries, and our churches need to do more in providing guidance essential to assist children and young people in coping with present-day permissiveness. To be sure, there are some encouraging things happening in the print and broadcast media that reflect a growing sensitivity on the parts of media management and the entertainment industry decision-makers regarding the appropriateness of what many refer to as "adult" entertainment and publications. Chapter IX speaks additionally to this subject.

As we view the present many-faceted decline in our nation's moral and spiritual values, no area demonstrates more how far we have fallen than does the sexual behavior of many. Essential to the propagation of the human race and ordained by our Creator as one of the greatest privileges and joys of marriage, America's sexual behavior has become a jungle of the lowest conceivable behavior. (No, I should not use the word "jungle," for in some ways the creatures of the jungle, acting instinctively, behave more responsibly than do many human beings who are endowed, supposedly, with higher abilities to discern the difference between right and wrong.)

Much of what we read and hear relative to sexual behavior pertains to teenagers and their practices. Writing in the May 19, 1997 issue of *U.S. News and World Report* (41), David Whitman has observed, however, that these problems exist beyond the young. He noted:

> Adult premarital sex is the "sin" Americans wink at. But if you think casual sex is a problem only for teenagers, take a look at the numbers for grown-ups (41).

In his article, Mr. Whitman referred to a book entitled *Marriage Savers* (42), written by Michael McManus. It is a book that I, as the author of *The Best of Mind and Spirit*, recommend to both those contemplating marriage and to those who are married.

Also mentioned by Whitman is the statement by Bishop James McHugh (43), the bishop of Camden, N.J., that "all sexual activity outside of marriage is wrong and has no moral justification."

Again, we are reminded of the need for homes and churches to assume responsibility for values education, including (and especially) sex education. But many parents and members of the clergy are unable or unwilling to take responsibility for this all-important and sacred duty of home and church. It follows then that sex education for many young people is acquired in other venues, such as the through "no questions asked" wholesale distribution of condoms instead of through helpful counsel by qualified, knowledgeable, and concerned counselors able to present sound, acceptable reasons for deferring sex until there is physical, economic, and spiritual readiness.

For those who react negatively to the latter approach, saying, "Such is out of the question, in view of the multitude of people involved," I can only add that ways must, and can be found to alleviate, in responsible ways, the psychologically and spiritually destructive sexual practices of our times. Certainly, a monumental challenge faces us; and with many people continuing to promote such ill-advised practices as the indiscriminate distribution of condoms, the task is not made easier. There are, however, some encouraging developments. The need for abstinence is increasingly receiving attention. It is encouraging to note, for example, that USA government sources declared recently that a portion of a five-year federal grant for sex education programs totaling $50,000,000 must be used for "abstinence-only" programs.

Stephanie Salter, a columnist for the *San Francisco Examiner* (44) raised the question in a November, 1997 column, "Could sex education be working?" She noted:

> The Atlanta-based program called Postponing Sex Involvement is one of the most successful. Developed in the early '80s, the abstinence-option program is presented to all eighth-grade Atlanta students. Using teen-agers in skits and hypothetical scenarios, the program has produced teens who are as much as 15 times less likely to have sex than teens who have not taken the course (44).

As indicated by the title of this volume, in the writing thus far and in subsequent chapters, the sexual and other problems contributing to the decline in our nation's moral and spiritual values can be brought closer to solution as the best of education and the best of religion are brought to bear upon them. Certainly, regarding teen-age sexual problems, responsible sex education by parents is especially needed. For many, parental "tough love" is called for. As one mother (presumably "tongue in cheek") indicated to her daughter: "If you engage in pre-marital sex, we'll kill you!—And, by the way, we love you very much!" Also, the powerful commandment, "Thou shall not commit adultery," from the Bible needs to be emphasized in the home as well as in the guidance of people both young and old.

A discussion of present sexual behaviors leads directly to a discussion of abortion, without doubt the most tragic of all sexually related problems. So much is being spoken and written in stating the differences between pro-lifers and those who support abortion.

In a highly insightful discussion of the matter in the January 12, 1998 issue of *Christianity Today* (45) Frederica Mathewes-Green, a former pro-abortionist, shared her thoughts relative to "Wanted: A New Pro-Life Strategy."[h] Some selected quotations and comments of others follow:

> January 22 marks a grim anniversary: 25 years since Roe v. Wade legalized abortion.
>
> Abortion has been a disaster, first for the children who died and second for those who survived to grieve a lost child, grandchild, or sibling. It has damaged us all. How can we even measure the spiritual cost levied on a country that pronounces the killing of its own children a celebrated right? It is tempting to avoid thinking about it, and when we do think of it, it is tempting to stew in helpless fury (45).
>
> Avoidance and fury—neither response has pushed us forward. As a movement, the pro-life cause has stopped. We are stuck, mired, at an impasse. We have had small gains and small losses, but the bottom line is the same: 1.5 million abortions a year. I suggest we use this morbid anniversary as an opportunity to reassess our strategy (45).

The author did come up with a strategy based, first of all, on listening, followed by persuasion. A discussion of her proposed approach continues in Chapter IX, which presents suggestions in dealing with America's current decline in its moral and spiritual values.

Certainly, the substantial involvement of young people in the use of alcohol and drugs deserves our attention. In the January 26, 1998 issue of *U.S. News and World Report* (46), J. J. Thompson wrote an article entitled, "Plugging the Kegs." He noted surveys indicate that up to 85 percent of college students imbibe and nearly half drink heavily. Drinking, he said, is not only common but is done mainly to get drunk. "Binge drinking" is the defining term.

Additional attention to the drinking problem is given later in *The Best of Mind and Spirit.*

Whereas alcohol use is the major problem of college students, younger students at pre-college levels indulge more in the use of drugs. According to USA drug policy adviser General Barry McCaffrey in an August, 1997 AP release (47), there had been a 122 percent increase in the past year in the number of 12-year-olds who said they knew someone who used hard drugs such as cocaine or heroin. The survey was sponsored by the Commission on Substance Abuse Among America's Adolescents (48), a special research body of the National Center on Addiction and Substance Abuse at Columbia University.[i]

Joseph Califano, former USA Secretary of Health, Education and Welfare, who heads the National Center, observed on NBC's *Today* show that "the drug problem must be attacked locally" (49), adding,

> This is not a problem for Washington. This is a prob-
> lem for parents, for schools, for churches. Almost
> three-fourths of the kids—15-, 16- and 17-year-olds
> and their parents—say their schools are not drug
> free. A drug-free school in America is an oxymoron.
> We have to do something about that. We have to do
> it locally where the parents are, in the family, in the
> community. That's where the battle is going to be
> fought (49).

Once again the need for lead roles of homes and churches is underscored (along with the involvement of our schools as well as other contributing agencies) as we cope with alcohol and drug problems in the decline of our nation's moral and spiritual values.

The problems of young people in the times in which we live are many. An August 11, 1998, Associated Press release out of Washington, D.C. (50), reported the results of the Horatio Alger Association's annual survey relative to "The State of Our Nation's

Youth" (50). Among other observations are the following:

> While large numbers of American teenagers believe their opportunities are boundless in the 21st century, many are concerned about their safety at school right now (50).

> In a look at the attitudes and expectations of the millennial generation, young people who will spend most of their lives in the 21st century, the survey finds that many of today's students believe crime and violence are the greatest problems (50).

> At the same time, Generation 2000 finds racial tensions and discrimination and poverty and unemployment to be of far lesser concern (50).

The lead editorial in the August 17, 1998 issue of the *Tulsa World* (51) is entitled "Child Criminals." Included among the comments are the following:

> Americans have been stunned in recent years and months to learn that young teen-agers and even pre-teens are capable of heinous and vicious crimes (51).

Also,

> We shake our heads, debate with our friends and wonder: Is it too much television and too little parental involvement? Has society just degenerated that much? Could it be some form of brain damage? Abuse and neglect? (51).

In the July 24, 1998 issue of *The Chronicle of Higher Education* (52) are observations entitled "Incivility in the Classroom Breeds 'Education Lite,'" by Paul A. Trout, associate professor of English at Montana State University at Bozeman. He observed:

> Ill-mannered, uncivil students are certainly nothing

new to higher education—remember the '60s? But over the last decade or so, the number of them on some campuses and in some classrooms has apparently reached a critical mass, provoking professors from across the country—and the political spectrum—to complain about them publicly (52).

In many discussions about problems of young people today, there is acknowledgment of the great need for values education in the home. Throughout this volume, attention is given to the traditional lead roles of homes and churches in values education of the young. Also, this book emphasizes the need for all of America's people and all of its concerned agencies (including its public schools at all levels) to join with and to be supportive of homes and churches in the strengthening of their roles. Additional discussion of other efforts that give promise of assisting young people in dealing with problems confronting them continues in Chapter IX.

Before leaving Chapter II with its considerable attention to various negative forces and their impact in shaping the lives of young people, I would hasten to point out that not all of them have been adversely influenced. Actually, in my observing of students through the years, I would note that there continue to be many young people of the highest level of citizenship and commitment to serving others. Largely because of their favorable home and church experiences, they have been able to withstand the negative forces at work in America's current decline in its moral and spiritual values. They have become strong in the process and can be powerful forces in alleviating the present problems of those who have not been so richly blessed.

We hear much about peer pressure, mostly about its negative nature. In Chapter IX, I propose that there be a reversal in application of peer pressure, with those who are secure and strong in their values leading those who have had little or no values guidance and are struggling and in need of help.

Chapter III

Education and Religion, Our Two Best Hopes: Their Differences and Compatibility

    Having noted in Chapter II some of the problems that reflect our nation's decline in its moral and spiritual values, what <u>can</u> and <u>may</u> we do? As indicated by the title of this volume, I believe that education and religion, as the two most powerful influences in shaping individuals and nations, hold the keys to coping with our present values' malaise.

    Whatever is done, of course, must recognize the need for homes and churches to continue, to the highest level possible, to be the lead agencies in values education of our children and young people. Schools need not and must not take over the basic responsibilities of homes and churches. They must, however, in view of the present decline in home and church influence, <u>become much more involved in and supportive of values education</u> provided by the two traditional lead agencies. Without public school support, great numbers of young people will be denied orientation to the values that are so essential to the good life of our citizens and our nation.

    As previously stated, this volume, which is written by an educator, goes beyond the commonly understood role of education with its three-pronged emphasis on the search for, the sharing of,

39

and the application of knowledge. With our nation in a moral and spiritual values crisis, this is a book written for all Americans concerned with the quality of education of their young people and the quality of life in America. It recommends the coming together of <u>education</u> and <u>religion</u> in dealing with American's values decline.

With the increased secularization of public education during the 20th century, the prevailing attitude and practice has become essentially that of keeping religion "on the sidelines." In view of the lessening of the traditional lead roles of homes and churches in providing values education for young people, however, the time has come for public schools to once again assume greater responsibility for values education, concurrent with academic learnings—not to replace homes and churches in their lead roles, but to <u>support them</u> in assuring <u>the best of both mind and spirit</u> for the masses of young people, many of whom are being denied such today.

Chapters VII and VIII deal with how education and religion <u>working in unison</u> can contribute to values education beyond what homes and churches are now doing, without violation of the conditions of the First Amendment. There is much that teachers, counselors, administrators, and school boards can do locally. And those in regional and national lead roles in education can have a tremendous impact if, without hesitation or apology, they will acknowledge the high roles of both education and religion in emphasizing <u>the best of mind and spirit</u> values in the total education of students.

"Religion" is defined in many ways. In its most general sense, it may be defined in terms of "that to which we give our primary attention and loyalty in life"—such as "making money," or "worship" of sports. David Elton Trueblood, Quaker theologian, in his book *Philosophy of Religion* (53), has stated:

> Fundamental to all religion is the experience of commitment or dedication. In its fullest and most mature form this is commitment to the will of God,

40

but, because there are many levels of religious development, it may be commitment to lesser objects (53), (p. 11).

George Galloway, British philosopher and theologian, in his book *Studies in the Philosophy of Religion* (54), has observed the following:

Only through the value realized in experience can we give positive spiritual content to the idea of Him who is the living Source and the abiding Ground of all truth and goodness (54), (p. 38).

William Temple, Archbishop of Canterbuy, in his volume *Nature, Man, and God* (55), wrote:

The heart of Religion is not an opinion about God, such as Philosophy might reach as the conclusion of its argument; it is a personal relationship with God (55), (p. 54).

The *Oxford Dictionary* notes that religion is:

. . . recognition on the part of man of some unseen higher power as having control of his destiny and as being entitled to obedience, reverence, and worship.

In *Webster's New Collegiate Dictionary*, religion is defined as:

. . . the service and worship of God or the supernatural.

At this point, let us consider how the term "religion" is understood and used in this volume. Three major monotheistic world religions (Christianity, Judaism, and Islam) share a common ancestor, Abraham. They all worship a living God; and all have in common, to a degree, their understandings of what is right and wrong. Many of the world's religions, including the three just mentioned as well as Hinduism, Buddhism, Confucianism, Zoroastrianism, Taoism, and others, subscribe in some measure to the Golden

Rule.

In this volume, "religion" will for the most part be used in a general sense. On some occasions, however, its usage may be more specific in referring to but one of a general grouping. As used in this volume, "religion" has reference to the best and the highest of human expression and behavior. I have chosen, in fact, to use the word "spirit" rather than the word "religion" in the title of this book in that it reflects more specifically the spiritual emphasis of this volume. To be sure, the word spirit itself has different meanings. In many religious faiths, including mine, it acknowledges God, the Supreme Being, as Spirit, along with the reality of the spiritual dimension in human existence.

In the March 5, 1999 issue of *The United Methodist Review* (56), Bishop Bruce P. Blake of the Oklahoma Methodist Area, observed that "Spirituality Is All Encompassing."[h] He stated:

> It is fascinating to me how often the word *spiritual* is used today in the life of the church. I am fascinated because I experience it being used in a variety of ways with a variety of meanings.
>
> Often the reference to *spiritual* represents a part of the life of a community or individual. This reference sets the spiritual over against or set apart from the remaining part of the life of a community or individual. I am increasingly uncomfortable with this use of the term.
>
> I do not experience the spiritual to be a segment of life. Spiritual formation does not mean forming a part of my existence. Rather, spirituality has to do with every part of my existence. Spiritual formation is the shaping of human existence in the light of the journey of faith. Nothing is excluded from being shaped.
>
> It has been said, "Spirituality is a special function

and a part of every function." Nothing is excluded from being shaped. "Spirituality is the integration of prayer and daily living," is another way of saying nothing is excluded from being shaped.

As I reflect on the life and teachings of Christ, there is no indication that spirituality is a segment or component of life. Rather, spirituality is a way of living every part of one's existence.

This understanding of spirituality is empowering, for it depends on a person's willingness to be open to the guidance of the Divine Spirit in all of life, the private closets of our existence, as well as our relationships and our public behavior. This understanding is helping me be certain that I do not consider myself to be *spiritually accomplished* when one component of my life is synchronized with the Divine. Rather, I live with the challenge that all my life is to be synchronized with the Divine (56).

It has been my observation that those of other faiths who come to the USA to study and/or to gain citizenship genuinely appreciate the freedom America offers to them to worship as they choose. And I would add that very few complain when those of the traditional Christian and Jewish faiths in America speak of God and invoke His blessings and guidance. Neither do they minimize the strong Judeo-Christian influence at the time of the founding of the great American democracy whose way of life they have coveted through the years and to which they have come to enjoy its freedom and to pledge their loyalty. Those who have achieved USA citizenship join with other Americans, in pledging allegiance to the USA flag, and in acknowledging their new home as "a nation under God."

In my associations over a period of years with those of differing faiths, it has been my experience that there is considerable interest in and support of each other's religious beliefs, regardless of our differences. The spiritual dimension of life is a reality among most peoples. The search for meaning in life is a reality; and this leads to identification with a Supreme Being.

I have observed considerable bonding among those of different faiths, especially among those who are secure in their religious beliefs. There are some, however, who choose to place primary emphasis on the differences among those of various faiths rather than on the considerable rapport we enjoy.

As is discussed in greater detail in Chapter VII, the "free marketplace" for all religious groups must exist in America's public schools and on its higher public education campuses, as is guaranteed by the First Amendment of the USA Constitution. (This, however, is not true of all nations, including some where Communism still rules.)

As we consider a sharing of education and religion in efforts to reverse the present decline in America's moral and spiritual values, it is well that attention be given to differences in understandings of education and religion, as well as to their compatibility. We must consider the fact that science, the "scientific method," and the "scientific point of view," are essential components of education. Further, there are differences among some of religious faith and some who are scientists; and there are differences within the ranks of each of the two groups. I would observe, additionally, that there are many of deep religious faith who are scientists, and many scientists who are deeply religious, as discussed in Chapter II. Additional attention is given to the differences between education and religion (as well as to their compatibility) in the immediate pages that follow. Also, some additional thoughts are shared in the closing pages of Chapter IX.

As noted in Chapter I, the overview chapter, education is understood by many people as being an enterprise separate from religion. Religion's role, as defined and used in this volume, however, is largely one of providing meaning and direction in the uses and applications of the vast body of knowledge now available (as well as the abundance of new knowledge to be revealed, as the result of educational and research efforts).

It is religion that gives the greatest meaning to life. In my own faith, Jesus' statement that "I am come that they might have life, and that they might have it more abundantly" (John 10:10), is especially meaningful. It is my religious faith that sets behavior standards for me based on love and on respect for the fact that people are the highest of God's creations, who are charged, in turn, to be good stewards of all of creation. It is my religious faith that leads me to think of each person (whatever his or her nationality, religious faith, color of skin, or socioeconomic status may be) as very important—as a child of God, and as a neighbor of mine.

David Sarnoff (57), born in Russia and an American radio executive, has observed the following in Bernard Mandelbaum's volume entitled *Choose Life* (11):

> In addition to engineers, the world of tomorrow will also need men and women with deep roots in our moral and spiritual heritage. "It is not brains that matter most," Dostoevski once wrote, "but that which guides them—the character, the heart, the generous qualities."
>
> Surely, it was never the Creator's design that humanity be subordinated to the machine. We cannot program a machine to know good or evil, or to be responsible for the social implications of its performance.
>
> In the midst of vast changes imposed by technology, the student will find that one element remains unchanged—the spiritual and moral inheritance given to him by his family, his church, and his college. This is what gives purpose and meaning to his endeavors (11), (p. 8).

In his book *Science in Search of God* (58), Kirtley F. Mather, Professor of Geology at Harvard University has noted:

Science has as its goal the complete description of the universe in which we live; religion seeks to find the most abundant life which man may possess in such a universe. Geology is a collection of beliefs and ideas about the earth; it deals with facts and experiences pertaining to the transformations of material objects when acted upon by such forces as gravitative attraction and electromagnetic impulses; it strives to interpret aright the world of sense perception, of which we are so constantly aware. Theology is a collection of beliefs and ideas about the mutual relations between God and man; it should deal with facts and experiences pertaining to the higher reaches of human life; it must strive to interpret aright the spiritual realities of which adventurous souls are abundantly aware (58), (pp. 43, 44).

Additionally, in another of his books entitled *Crusade for Life* (59), Mather has observed:

Whereas science attempts to describe the world and man as they now are, religion attempts to describe the world and man as they might be. It seeks for directives that will guide men to use the power and the techniques provided by science in ways that will promote the transformation of man and society toward the goal that it envisions. It calls for value judgments rather than statistics of measurements. It deals with purposes and motives as well as causes and results. It is concerned with the part of reality which is forever beyond the ken of science (59), (pp. 22, 23).

In a book written by Edward R. Murrow and edited by Edward P. Morgan, entitled *This I Believe* (60),(i) Herbert Hoover, President of the United States of America, 1929-1933 (61), (and a great humanitarian who turned over his entire salary to charity) wrote:

> My professional training was in science and engineering. That is a training in the search for truth and its application to the use of mankind. With the growth of science we have had a continuous contention from a tribe of atheistic and agnostic philosophers that there is an implacable conflict between science and religion in which religion will be vanquished. I do not believe it.
>
> I believe not only that religious faith will be victorious, but that it is vital to mankind that it shall be. We may differ in form and particulars in our religious faith. Those are matters which are sacred to each of our inner sanctuaries. It is our privilege to decline to argue them. Their real demonstration is the lives that we live (61).

President Hoover continued:[k]

> From their religious faith, the Founding Fathers enunciated the most fundamental law of human progress since the Sermon on the Mount, when they stated that man received from the Creator certain inalienable rights and that these rights should be protected from the encroachment of others by law and justice (61).

And he added:

> Always growing societies record their faith in God; decaying societies lack faith and deny God. But America is not a decaying society. It remains strong. Its faith is in compassion and in God's intelligent mercy (61), (60), (pp. 75, 76).

Some argue that religious faith has no place in academia because it is too subjective—that religion cannot "stand up" against scientific inquiry and reason. In his book entitled *Not Minds Alone* (16), Kenneth Irving Brown observed:

> Jacque Maritain (62), when asked if his allegiance to the Roman Catholic Church did not close certain doors to complete philosophic and religious inquiry, is reported to have made unequivocal answer: He said that he was a loyal Catholic, but that his religious faith in no way limited or impaired his freedom of scholastic inquiry (16), (62), (pp. 44, 45).

Brown also quoted Howard Lowry from Lowry's book *The Mind's Adventure* (63), in which Lowry stated:

> "The committed Christian surrenders a certain freedom of action," he writes. But, he does not lose his freedom of inquiry. The allegiance he gives is to One in whose service there is "perfect freedom." This includes the right to reason, to investigation, to critical judgments. The Christian can hold with Socrates that the unexamined life is not worth living. But he insists that the examination be complete—that man be studied in a perspective that includes his highest aspirations and insights (16), (63), (p. 83).

Religion is largely a matter of belief, trust, and faith in relationship to a Higher Being—a relationship of the highest level of love and obedience.

Oswald Chambers in his book *My Utmost For His Highest* (64), has stated:

> Belief is not an intellectual act; belief is a moral act whereby I deliberately commit myself. My relationship to God is a personal one, not an intellectual one (64), (p. 357).

Education is largely an intellectual endeavor with emphases on reason and logic. Education and religion are different in some ways, to be sure, but they are also compatible. Contrary to the thinking of some, the intellectual process and reason are, to a degree, "at home" in religion.

In the book of Isaiah of the Bible we read:

> Come now, and let us reason together, saith the Lord: though your sins be as scarlet, they shall be as white as snow; though they be red like crimson, they shall be as wool (Isaiah 1:18).

On October 16, 1998, the *Tulsa World* published an Associated Press story by Victor L. Simpson entitled, "Pope Defends Church's 'Values'" (65). On the occasion of his 20th anniversary as Pope, Pope John Paul spoke out in an "encyclical," one of the most important documents a pope can issue. Simpson summarized the Pope's presentation as follows:

> The encyclical is titled "Fides et Ratio," Latin for "Faith and Reason," and grapples with the issue of religion in the modern world, when expectations have been raised by scientific and technological progress. It stresses that faith and reason are not incompatible.
>
> He said mankind has always asked questions such as, "Who am I? Where have I come from and where am I going? Why is there evil? What is there after this life?"
>
> But today some Catholics risk "losing their way in the shifting sands of widespread skepticism" while "many people stumble through life to the very edge of the abyss without knowing where they are going," John Paul said.
>
> "At times, this happens because those whose vocation is to give cultural expression to their thinking no longer look to the truth, preferring quick success to the toil of patient inquiry into what makes life

worth living."

The encyclical was in effect a call to action for the proper education of Catholics.

John Paul said he encouraged scientific progress but it "should be wedded to the philosophical and ethical values which are the distinctive and indelible mark of the human being" (65).

It should be noted also that the gift of faith is not restricted only to a few, but is available to all who will accept it, as indicated in II Peter of the Bible (II Peter 3:9).

Actually, the best of both education and religion is necessary to achieve completeness and fullness of life.

As quoted in Rabbi Bernard Mandelbaum's book entitled *Choose Life* (11), Mahatma Gandhi, great Hindu nationalist leader of India, once observed:

If we could solve all the mysteries of the Universe, we would be coequal with God. Every drop of ocean shares its glory, but is not the ocean (66), (11), (p. 19).

And Jesus said, "Man shall not live by bread alone, but by every word that proceedeth out of the mouth of God" (Matthew 4:4).

In 1958, I was privileged to participate in a national conference on "Religion and the State University" on the campus of the University of Michigan. Although no "official point of view" was presented, that which was shared and discussed at the conference continues to have meaning for educators today. Drawing from the Introduction to the summary-volume (of the same name as the conference) (67), edited by Erich A. Walter (formerly Dean of Students at the University of Michigan and later the Assistant to the President at the university), are observations by some of the speakers at the conference.[l]

Walton Bean (68), Professor of History at the University of California at Berkeley, spoke regarding "What is the State

University?" He discussed the dual aspects of a state university as "a community of scholars and as a place where young people develop their purposes in life" (67), (pp. 58-69).

Following are comments of other participants.

Paul Kauper (69), Professor of Law at the University of Michigan and a member of the Board of Higher Education of the American Lutheran Church, spoke of "Law and Public Opinion" (67), observing:

> In view of the place that religion has occupied and continues to occupy in the life and history of man, its influence in the shaping of ideas, its impact on culture and its significance as a unifying and integrating force that provides a high sense of purpose and motivation and opens new vistas of truth, goodness, and beauty, religion must of necessity command some attention at any academic institution both as an intellectual discipline and as a way of life. The university may well take the position that it is derelict to the high purpose for which it was created if it fails to deal in a positive way with religion as a vital force in the life and history of man. Indeed, it is fair to assert that for a university deliberately to exclude from its curriculum all courses with a positive religious content is not simply to fail to teach religion but in itself becomes a telling witness that religion is irrelevant to that process of cultivating the mind and spirit that we call higher education (67), (pp. 69-86).

Helen White (70), Professor of English and Chair of the Department of English at the University of Wisconsin, discussed the place of religion as a branch of learning as "one of the great humanities" (67), (pp. 89-105).

Other speakers included:

Mark Ingraham (71), Professor of Mathematics and Dean of

the College of Letters and Sciences at the University of Wisconsin (as well as a former president of the American Association of University Professors), explored the question of academic freedom, including the professor's and the student's right to express religious views, in and out of the classroom (67), (pp. 106-119).

George Shuster (72), President of Hunter College and author of *The Catholic Spirit in America; Religion and Education*, pleaded for instruction in religion to be at the same high level of intellectual activity as the student receives in professional studies (67), (pp. 172-191).

Subsequent commentary relative to the 1958 University of Michigan Conference appeared in the March-April 1959 issue of the publication entitled *Religious Education* (73). Special attention was given to the need for encouraging students in their religious experiences and growth.

I would acknowledge, at this point, that the academic function is what makes education unique among the various agencies of society; but as emphasized throughout this volume, it is not (and must not be) the sole function of education.

In calling for a stronger supportive role of values education by those of us in public education (pre-school through doctoral study), I would underscore again that there is no intent to reduce emphasis on academic programs. To the contrary, as a life-long educator and behavioral scientist, I am committed to the strengthening of traditional academics, as well as newly developing programs of instruction, research, outreach, and service.

The fact is, however, that academic programs (especially research and technology) have in many areas, progressed well beyond the abilities of most people to understand and to use wisely their abundance of findings and "know how."

Consider also, the following statement of Sir Walter Moberly in his book, *The Crisis in the University* (74):

> But what should he do with his chemistry or languages when he has acquired them, whether and why injustice and cruelty and fraud are bad and their

opposites good, whether faith in God is a snare and a delusion or is the only basis on which human life can be lived without disaster—all these things the student must find out for himself as best he may, for a university education can do nothing to help him.

If you want a bomb, the chemistry department will teach you how to build it; if you want a healthy body, the departments of physiology and medicine will teach you how to tend it. But when you ask whether and why you should want bombs or cathedrals or healthy bodies, the university, on this view, must be content to be dumb and impotent. It can give help and guidance in all things subsidiary but not in the attainment of the one thing needful. In living their lives, the younger are left "the sport of every random gust." <u>But for the educator this is abdication</u> (74), (pp. 51, 52).

In concluding this chapter, I would acknowledge that education and religion are different, yet they are compatible. Both are essential in our efforts to reverse the current decline in our nation's moral and spiritual values. Both are essential in achieving and maintaining the good life of our nation and its citizens.

Chapter IV

Some Public Education Associations and Their Publications Dealing with Moral and Spiritual Matters

Attention has been given already to the founding bases of our nation. From these premises a democratic way of life has emerged which, despite our current problems, continues to be the envy of other nations of the world. Especially significant has been the development of educational opportunities in its public schools for all people of America.

The first of several educational developments, to be discussed in the pages that follow, is the passage of the Morrill Act, originated by Congressman Justin Morrill of Vermont, and signed into law by President Abraham Lincoln in 1862—an Act that made available public lands for the establishment and support of "industrial and agricultural education." From this legislation came the great land-grant higher education institutions of America, to supplement existing privately supported higher education institutions and a small number of publicly-supported colleges which existed primarily to serve men of wealth, in the fields of medicine, law, theology, and the liberal arts.

The mission of the new land-grant institutions essentially was "to serve the sons and the daughters of the working classes, in the study of the practical arts, but not to the exclusion of the liberal arts." The Morrill Act gave dignity to all worthwhile labor, opened the opportunities of higher education to all, and underscored the importance of preparing students to both make a good living and to have a good life. I have been privileged to have had nearly a half century of rich association with land-grant universities.[m]

The Morrill Act of 1862 was but the first of a series of developments consistent with the democratic spirit of the Morrill Act. The Hatch Act of 1887 provided for research support; the Second Morrill Act of 1890 provided for equitable distribution of funds to both black and white land-grant institutions, and the Smith-Lever Act of 1914 established support for extension services. In October of 1994, the U.S. Congress passed legislation conferring land-grant status on 29 Native American tribal colleges; and in January 1995 the American Indian Higher Education Consortium (AIHEC) became a member of the National Association of State Universities and Land-Grant Colleges.

The outstanding leadership and service of the National Association of State Universities and Land-Grant Colleges continues, consistent with its commitment to be relevant to the times and the needs of the nation and its citizens. Recently completed is the NASULGC initiative to study the future of public universities in the USA (3). In 1995, the NASULGC sought the support of the W.K. Kellogg Foundation to assist in this effort (3). The Foundation agreed both to support a multi-year national commission to rethink the role of public higher education in the United States and to lend its name to the effort. The Commission announced a plan to issue a series of five letters (reports) to the presidents and chancellors of State Universities and Land-Grant Colleges in the USA, one each on the subjects of "Student Experiences," "Access," "Engaged Institutions," "A Learning Society," and "Campus Culture." The first of the five publications, entitled *Returning to Our Roots—The Student Experience* (3), was published in 1997. Among points of emphasis (and especially relevant to this volume) is a statement by the Kellogg Commission:

> Values deserve special attention in this effort. The
> biggest educational challenge we face revolves

around developing character, conscience, citizen-ship, tolerance, civility, and individual and social responsibility in our students. We must not ignore this obligation in a society that sometimes gives the impression that virtues such as these are discre-tionary. These should be standard equipment, not options, in our graduates (3).

The Commission also noted, in discussing "healthy learning environments" that:

If there is a more unhealthy factor on campus today than excessive consumption of alcohol, we cannot identify it. Both research and anecdotal evidence indicate that alcohol is often involved in the diffi-culties and tragedies students encounter. Part of creating a healthy environment is helping students understand that alcohol is a dangerous intoxicant which, if used at all, should be used in moderation (3).

The second of the five proposed Commission publications, dealing with "access" (3), was released in 1998, and the final three publications followed in 1999 and 2000.

At this point I would mention a recently published volume written by President Emeritus John R. Campbell of Oklahoma State University entitled *Reclaiming a Lost Heritage . . . Land-Grant and Other Higher Education Initiatives for the Twenty-First Century* (75). On July 16-17, 1998, Campbell participated in a Symposium on "The Life and Legacy of Justin Smith Morrill (1810-1898)," author of the Land-Grant Acts of 1862 and 1890, where he presented a paper entitled, "Empowering Land-Grant Colleges and Universities for the Twenty-first Century." Quoting from his book, he noted that "the peoples' colleges and universities" (as Land-Grant institutions have become known) are becoming less and less accessible to many for which they were created to serve. He noted, additionally, that high costs (together with the inability of growing numbers of students to qualify for financial assistance) and less relevance of many programs to the needs of society (leading to the loss of public support) are also of great concern.

Contributing much to my orientation and preparation as an educator, has been the American Council on Education and its publication entitled, *The Student Personnel Point of View* (4), first issued as a pamphlet in 1938 and published with some revisions in 1949. It has meant more to me in the shaping of my educational philosophy and commitment than has any other single educational publication.

Members of the American Council on Education's Committee on Student Personnel Work, who revised the original brochure and produced the 1949 publication, were E. G. Williamson, Chairman, Willard W. Blaesser, Helen D. Bragdon, William S. Carlson, W. H. Cowley, D. D. Feder, Helen G. Fisk, Forrest H. Kirkpatrick, Esther Lloyd-Jones, T. R. McConnell, Thornton W. Merriam, and Donald J. Shank.

George F. Zook, President of the American Council on Education, on June 1, 1949 (4), wrote in the Foreword of *The Student Personnel Point of View* (4) the following:

> In 1937 The American Council on Education held a two-day conference on problems related to the clarification of the field of student personnel work, the relationship of student personnel work to other phases of institutional programs, and the need for research and special studies to determine the nature and direction of future developments in student personnel work. The report of this conference was published under the title *The Student Personnel Point of View*. For many years prior to this conference the Council had taken an active interest in the field of student personnel work, and as early as 1926 had published a report of a survey made by L. B. Hopkins. Special consideration had also been given to this area by several Council committees, among

them the Committee on Personnel Methods and its successor, the Committee on Measurement and Guidance.

The Student Personnel Point of View constituted a distinct contribution in the personnel field; first, because it delimited personnel activities from other administrative and instructional functions more clearly than had any previous statement; second, because it stressed the importance of coordinating various types of personnel services; third, because it pointed the way for future studies and special brochures; and fourth, because it led to the appointment by the Council of its Committee on Student Personnel Work, which has been responsible for the preparation of a number of important brochures.

The 1949 ACE Committee on Student Personnel Work produced a revised brochure of *The Student Personnel Point of View* (4), in which it emphasized, first:

The development of students as whole persons interacting in social situations is the central concern of student personnel work and of other agencies of education (4), (p. 1);

and second:

The concept of education is broadened to include attention to the student's well-rounded development—physically, socially, emotionally, and spiritually, as well as intellectually (4), (p. 1).

Emphasizing that the student personnel point of view holds that the major responsibility for a student's growth in personal and social wisdom rests with the student himself, nevertheless, various institutional personnel services to aid, as necessary, were proposed, together with comments about the administration of the services. Also, the need for <u>evaluation of services</u> and of a research emphasis was underscored. In many ways the ACE publication continues to be as meaningful and as valid today as it was a half century ago.[n]

Somewhat coincidentally but more importantly, indicative of a shared concern and commitment of the two great American higher education associations that have had special meaning for me and for many other educators (the National Association of State Universities and Land-Grant Colleges, and the American Council on Education), both have recently singled out for special attention the subject of student values. Reference has already been made to the 1995 National Association of State Universities and Land-Grant Colleges' initiative to study the future of state and land-grant universities, along with the formation of the Kellogg Commission on the Future of State and Land-Grant Universities to conduct the study. Also, references have been made to the first two of five publications of the Commission, the 1997 document entitled *Returning to Our Roots: The Student Experience* (3), in which it is noted that "the biggest educational challenge we face revolves around developing character, conscience, citizenship, tolerance and individual and social responsibility in our students," and the 1998 publication regarding "access" (3).

About the same time that the National Association of State Universities and Land-Grant Colleges was beginning its study of public higher education in America, the American Council on Education was at work on a special issue of its magazine, *Educational Record* (5), devoted totally to the subject of "College and Character: Preparing Students for Lives of Civic Responsibility." As the Summer/Fall, 1997 issue, it was the final publication of *Educational Record*, in that the American Council on Education had plans to replace it with a new magazine. Wendy Bresler, Editor-in-Chief, noted (5):

> The very same conversations about character, civic education, and moral leadership with which our authors grapple in this last issue of *Educational Record* have filled the pages since its inception 78 years ago.

And she added:

> As recently as 1992, we focused an entire issue on "The University as Citizen: A Mission to Serve."

Stanley O. Ikenberry, ACE President, in his introductory statement to the special issue entitled, "Values, Character, Leadership: Reexamining our Mission" (5), made the following observations:

> At its best, higher education is concerned with more than knowledge and facts . . . We expect our students to both understand and embrace the values and ethical principles of the profession or field they have chosen. We know that higher education can change lives. We believe college graduates are different for having gone to college, because if we have done our jobs, they will possess values, character, and wisdom. Though more difficult to define, these characteristics ultimately are the more important goals of higher education. For whatever combination of reasons, a broader public agenda that is concerned with values, civic life, the common good, and related questions is challenging us to think more carefully about higher education's ultimate purposes . . . In this issue of *Educational Record*, our distinguished authors contend with both broad and specific issues surrounding the college campus and its role in character education . . . . It is about time, after half a century of focusing on campus growth, specialized professions, and the transmission of information, for higher education to broaden the discussion to include some of the intangible, more difficult to define qualities of what it means to be an "educated person." In part, the demand for this may be driven by the decline in the quality of civic life in the larger society and by a concern that colleges can and should do something about it. In part,

the discussion also is fueled by technology: The virtual university may well be able to deliver information, some argue, but there must be more to higher education than the assimilation of information (5).

Both the NASULGC statement entitled "Returning to Our Roots—The Student Experience" (3), and the ACE publication about "College and Character: Preparing Students for Lives of Civic Responsibility" (5), are highly student-oriented. There is much to be gained from the study of both presentations.

The contents of the ACE publication relate largely to what can be done in the development of character and responsibility in students and in student relationships with each other. Of particular relevance in the special issue of the ACE's *Educational Record* (5) are: "The Power of Peer Culture" by Jon C. Dalton and Anne Marie Petrie (76), and "Religious Faith and the Development of Character on Campus" by William H. Willimon (14).

Earlier in this chapter, in sharing the present concerns of the National Association of State Universities and Land-Grant Colleges about the needs and problems of higher education today and in the future, it was noted that in the first of five NASULGC reports of their study entitled *Returning to Our Roots—The Student Experience* (3), considerable attention is given to discussing the drinking problems of students. Again, it is significant that the American Council on Education, acting independently, has also been at work on how to deal with the drinking problems of young people. In the September 14, 1998 issue of "Higher Education and National Affairs" (77), a second publication of the American Council on Education, was a report entitled "Task Force Releases Strategies to Reduce Alcohol Abuse." The report stated, in part:

> College students, parents, and higher education officials must work together to prevent the harm that alcohol abuse can cause the campus community, said participants of a Washington, DC press briefing last week concerning college drinking.

The Inter-Association Task Force on Alcohol and Other Substance Abuse Issues presented the media with a new kind of six-pack—"The Safety Six-Pack for Back-to-School 1998"—which outlines a series of actions and tips for parents, students, and colleges as the new academic year begins. The Task Force is a coalition of more than 20 higher education associations, including the American Council on Education (77).

Additional attention is given to the drinking problem (as well as to other problems of young people today) in Chapter IX.

Let us now move to another important ingredient in our considerations of what we can and must do to reverse America's current decline in its moral and spiritual values—the increased pluralism in America, (including in its schools). Chapter V gives attention to "International Dimensions."

Chapter V

International Dimensions

As the two great national education associations, the National Association of State Universities and Land-Grant Colleges and the American Council on Education, have contributed to my education, so have the opportunities I have enjoyed internationally. Some of the opportunities have been abroad, and some have been in our own land to which there has been a massive migration of people from throughout the world. It is the latter about which I wish to comment in this chapter, for with the coming to America of great numbers of peoples from other cultures and backgrounds, we have become more pluralistic, a reality which needs to be considered in this volume.

Before further consideration of "the great migration" to America, I would acknowledge that there have been some chapters in our becoming a great nation of which we cannot be proud. I would mention two: first, the failure of the early immigrants to America to respect the rights of its native inhabitants, and second, the cultural acceptance of slavery, especially of blacks. Certainly, we are grateful for steps taken subsequently to accord dignity and rights to descendants of those abused.

Having acknowledged the above, I would note that a land of rich resources and opportunities awaited those from abroad who began the migration more than 500 years ago to what is now the United States of America. Accelerating numbers (primarily from Europe and other western world nations) came to stay, to make a living, and to rear families—and I would add, to share in the continuing development of this great land of opportunity. More recently, especially in the latter half of the 20th Century, increasing numbers have come from the Near East, the Far East, and the Southern Hemisphere—some to become American citizens and others for study opportunities.

With the increased diversity of America's people, we have become, as previously mentioned, a more pluralistic nation. It is my belief that this great "coming together" of those from different backgrounds has made America an even greater nation. And yet, there have been, and there continue to be, problems as we strive "to form a more perfect union."

As the result of my involvements internationally, I have gained appreciations, understandings, and perspectives that are helpful in dealing with present problems, as well as assisting in our efforts of becoming a greater nation. Let me summarize some of these involvements which have, for the most part, furthered my love and respect for peoples throughout the world.

My international education began as a first generation American born of Swiss parentage from the German speaking sector of Switzerland. During my undergraduate and graduate years of college, there were increasing opportunities to meet and interact with students, teachers, and visiting speakers from other lands. A special privilege and learning experience for me was to room with a fellow graduate student from China in the summer of 1941 when I began my graduate studies at the University of Minnesota.

There followed an acceleration of international contacts and involvements after the completion of my doctoral study, with appointments to serve at Drake University, at Texas A&M University, and at Oklahoma State University, where for more than a half century my wife Maxine and I shared in a "feast" of international associations, travel, and service.

There have been the associations with tens of thousands of students from other nations during those years, along with involvements with increasing numbers of faculty and staff from abroad. Since coming to Oklahoma State University more than 40 years ago, some 80 to 125 different nations have been represented in each year's student body. We have loved the students from other lands, and they have returned that love, leading to our frequent sharing with them in celebrating their respective religious holidays, enjoying meals and other occasions, and interacting day-to-day, on and off campus. In turn, we have visited in the homes of some of the students from abroad, as we have traveled to their homelands.

Additionally, in the last half century, Oklahoma State University has been involved in education and development programs in more than 50 different nations of the world. The first program of USA President Harry S. Truman's post-World War II Point Four initiative was Oklahoma State University's 16-year technical assistance contract with the Kingdom of Ethiopia. Together with emphasis on agricultural development, there were also programs of assistance in a number of other areas, including the founding of a high school at Jimma, establishing a college at Alemaya, and developing a water system to serve many areas of the Kingdom of Ethiopia.

It has been my privilege to travel to some 50 different nations of the world and to spend time with people of those nations. There have been opportunities to lecture and to interact with students and faculty members in many of the places visited.

Providing me with new insights and understandings internationally was the opportunity to serve in the late '70s and early '80s as a member and chairman of the Board of Trustees of World Neighbors, Inc., an Oklahoma City-based "Helping People to Help Themselves" program.

In 1976 and 1977, I served as the USA ambassador to UNESCO, the United Nations Educational, Scientific, and Cultural Organization, based in Paris, France. In this highly diverse and often divided body (for the Soviet Union and its satellite nations were at the height of their power at the time and were formidable foes in UNESCO's world arena), there were abundant opportunities to meet and to interact with those of the 157 member nations at that time. The coffee breaks and a busy schedule of social events most evenings provided special opportunities to come to know each other. National and political differences were usually put aside on such occasions. One evening my counterpart from the Soviet Union and I were drinking orange juice and talking when our colleague from India walked by us. He stopped, shook his head, and observed, "I never thought I'd see the day when the representatives of the USA and the USSR would be drinking orange juice together!" The next day found us opposing each other on issues—perhaps in a somewhat friendlier way than usual, however, because of our visit the evening before.

For six weeks in 1976, UNESCO's World Conference was held in Nairobi, Kenya. I served initially as the vice chairman of the USA delegation, but due to the considerable absence of the chairman (a career diplomat in the USA State Department), the chairmanship of the USA delegation became my responsibility for the majority of the time. This afforded me some special opportunities for involvement with not only the official delegates, but also with observers from throughout the world. I was once again reminded how much the peoples of most nations of the world (and especially so-called developing nations) covet America's way of life.

I would add that our conversations were always in English, or through an interpreter. They had to be! As privileged as I have been in my formal education, I was dependent in most cases on the ability of those of other nations to speak my language. Actually, in that English increasingly is becoming a second language in so many countries, communications are greatly facilitated.

Although at a lesser level in my retirement years, I maintain associations with peoples of other lands. The considerable impact of earlier opportunities to be with those of other backgrounds— especially of different religious beliefs—is still very real and continues to be meaningful, including in the writing of this book. Because of the substantial presence of those from abroad in the

USA and because of their impact on what we think, what we do, who we are, and who we are becoming, this chapter about "International Dimensions" is included in *The Best of Mind and Spirit*.

Love is the key word in associating with others whether they are our next-door neighbors, or friends from other nations. The Apostle Paul, in the 13th Chapter of First Corinthians of the Bible (often referred to as the Love Chapter)[o] stated:

> Though I speak with the tongues of men and of angels, and have not charity, I am become as sounding brass, or a tinkling cymbal.
>
> And though I have the gift of prophecy, and understand all mysteries, and all knowledge; and though I have all faith, so that I could remove mountains; and have not charity, I am nothing.
>
> And though I bestow all my goods to feed the poor, and though I give my body to be burned, and have not charity, it profiteth me nothing.
>
> Charity suffereth long, and is kind; charity envieth not; charity vaunteth not itself, is not puffed up,
>
> Doth not behave itself unseemly, seeketh not her own, is not easily provoked, thinketh no evil;
>
> Rejoiceth not in iniquity, but rejoiceth in the truth;
>
> Beareth all things, believeth all things, hopeth all things, endureth all things.
>
> Charity never faileth: but whether there be prophecies, they shall fail; whether there be tongues, they shall cease; whether there be knowledge, it shall vanish away.
>
> For we know in part, and we prophesy in part.
>
> But when that which is perfect is come, then that

which is in part shall be done away.

When I was a child, I spake as a child, I understood as a child, I thought as a child: but when I became a man, I put away childish things.

For now we see through a glass, darkly; but then face to face: now I know in part; but then shall I know even as also I am known.

And now abideth faith, hope, charity, these three; but the greatest of these is charity (I Corinthians 13:1-13).

Actually, love is more of a common denominator in the feelings and attitudes among peoples of the world than is generally believed. As is mentioned a number of times in this volume, the Golden Rule, in some manner and to some degree, is lifted up and supported by many of the religions of the world, including the three great monotheistic religions, Christianity, Judaism, and Islam.

Dr. Karl Menninger, a psychiatrist and co-founder of the world-renowned Menninger Clinic in Topeka, Kansas, in his book *Whatever Became of Sin?* (78), spoke of sin and love, and of their relationship. Sin, he observed, is:

Behavior that violates the moral code or the individual conscience or both; behavior which pains or harms or destroys my neighbor—or me, myself (78), (p. 17).

Following is a prayer of love, attributed to Saint Francis of Assisi (79):

Lord, make me an instrument of Your Peace; where there is hatred, let me sow love; where there is injury, pardon; where there is doubt, faith; where there is despair, hope; where there is darkness, light; and where there is sadness, joy.

O Divine Master, grant that I may not so much seek to be consoled as to console; to be understood as to understand; to be loved as to love; for it is in giving that we receive, it is in pardoning that we are pardoned, and it is in dying that we are born to eternal life.

Norman Cousins, American editor and essayist (80) is quoted in Rabbi Bernard Mandelbaum's volume entitled *Choose Life* (11), as follows:

The major problem on earth is not the bomb. The bomb is actually the product of the problem. The main problem is that the human imagination has not yet expanded to the point where it comprehends its own essential unity. People are not yet aware of themselves as a single interdependent species requiring the proper performance of certain vital services if the human race is to be sustained. They have developed a world reach without a world consciousness (11), (p. 87).

Adlai Stevenson, American lawyer and diplomat, noted the following comments of two astronauts, one from the Soviet Union and one American, as they viewed the earth on their respective returns from space (81), also as presented in Mandelbaum's *Choose Life* (11):

"How beautiful is our earth!" exclaimed Major Gagarin as he came down from space in 1961 (11), (p. 85).

"Man, that view is tremendous!" shouted Colonel Glenn,[p] looking at the same view (11), (p. 85).

Adlai Stevenson commented additionally:

These two men have more in common than either has with the ideologists of conquest. This is not just Pollyanna talk. Wars start in the blind, angry hearts of men. But it is hard to hate those who toil and hope and discover beside you in a common human venture. The Glenns of our world could be new men in a quite new sense—the new men, who, having seen our little planet in a wholly new perspective, will be ready to accept as a profound spiritual insight the unity of mankind (11), (p. 86).

And, Martin Buber (82), Israeli philosopher, has stated, also in Mandelbaum's *Choose Life* (11):

After the heavenly sacred fact of being a child of God, nothing is as great in human existence as the earthly sacred fact of being a brother of men (11), (p. 74).

What privileges I have had in meeting, in coming to know, and in working with many of the peoples of the world. As an American citizen, I have enjoyed (along with other Americans) a favored relationship with those of many other lands because of the high regard worldwide, historically, for our nation's way of life. So many from abroad continue to believe that our democratic land of opportunity is "the greatest,"—which most Americans also continue to believe despite the monumental problems we face in reversing the decline in the moral and spiritual values of our nation.

There are those who believe that the growing diversity and the increased pluralism of the USA (due in part to the addition of those of other backgrounds) adds to the present decline in America's values. Instead of noting the many things we have in common that contribute to <u>community</u> among us, they choose to emphasize our differences. My experiences do not lead me to that conclusion. Most who come to America to become USA citizens or come for periods of study have proven to be good additions to those who are already citizens of America. This has been especially true when we who are established in our nation have made efforts to help newcomers feel welcome and at home. Where love, friendship, and goodwill have been expressed to our new neighbors whatever their nationality, religion, or color of skin may be a bonding often will have taken place. I have observed this especially in relation to our differing religious faiths. The fact that those who come to America are free to manifest fully their respective religious faiths in their new home nation is greatly appreciated. They are grateful that the United States of America has no state religion and that they are free to worship as they please. Most also honor the fact that this great democratic nation was founded on Judeo-Christian beliefs and principles—that the USA is "a nation under God." It is a mystery to many who have chosen to share in the blessings of America that some who have lived here for a longer time and have benefited most from this "nation under God" are among those who oppose any mention or acknowledgment of God in public life, including public schools.

Reference has been made to my years of association with World Neighbors, Inc., based in Oklahoma City, Oklahoma. Among the different words descriptive of the relationships I have enjoyed with those from other lands during my lifetime, I like best the word "neighbors."

In the Parable of the Good Samaritan Jesus was asked, "Who is my neighbor?" He answered:

> A certain man went down from Jerusalem to Jericho, and fell among thieves, which stripped him of his raiment, and wounded him, and departed, leaving him half dead.
>
> And by chance there came down a certain priest that way: and when he saw him, he passed by on the other side.
>
> And likewise a Levite, when he was at the place, came and looked on him, and passed by on the other side.
>
> But a certain Samaritan, as he journeyed, came

where he was: and when he saw him, he had compassion on him,

And went to him, and bound up his wounds, pouring in oil and wine, and set him on his own beast, and brought him to an inn, and took care of him.

And on the morrow when he departed, he took out two pence, and gave them to the host, and said unto him, "Take care of him; and whatsoever thou spendest more, when I come again, I will repay thee."

Which now of these three, thinkest thou, was neighbour unto him that fell among the thieves?

The one who originally asked the question "Who is my neighbor?" responded to Jesus' question as follows:

"He that shewed mercy on him."

Then Jesus admonished him:

"Go and do thou likewise" (Luke 10:30-37).

In many academic communities throughout America, there are off-campus programs that serve students from other lands in a "neighborly" way. One such program was underway when I arrived at Oklahoma State University in 1958. It was led by a wonderful Jewish lady, affectionately known by international students as "Mamma Levin." The wife of a distinguished Russian history scholar and teacher, Dr. Alfred Levin, she served full-time as a volunteer in helping students from other lands. She and like-minded "neighbors" established a comprehensive "host family" program that not only assisted her in her many labors, but also helped numbers of those from other lands feel at home in the USA.

Mamma Levin was an excellent cook, something students came to learn early in their associations with her. On one occasion, two students from abroad decided they would like to celebrate

Thanksgiving in the traditional American way with turkey and the trimmings. They asked Mrs. Levin if she would help them prepare the turkey. She was happy, as usual, to help, and asked them to bring the turkey to her home for preparation and baking—which they did. In fact, they brought <u>two birds</u>! One look at the carcasses, however, caused Mamma Levin to be suspicious. She recalled a news story from the previous day about the disappearance of two geese from the flock at Theta Pond on the OSU campus. She asked the students where they had secured the "turkeys." She had surmised quickly that before her were the remains of the two missing geese. After first maintaining they had purchased the birds at a local market, they wilted under Mrs. Levin's interrogation. Needless to say, when Mamma Levin finished chastising the students, there was no further disciplinary action needed other than to replace the two geese at Theta Pond. Later, as I recall, the guilty students were invited by the Levins for a belated Thanksgiving meal.

Of more recent vintage in the service of Oklahoma State University students from abroad, is the "Mission to Internationals, Inc." located close to campus. Tom Stewart, an ordained pastor, and his wife Liz, founded the MTII in 1980, and have served students ever since, providing such services and activities as practical help for new students, social events to establish friendships, weekly fellowship that includes games, singing and Bible studies, and weekly core group devotions on campus. Also a weekly visitation program, opportunities to attend conferences during school vacation periods, pastoral counseling, a host family program, regular correspondence with graduates, and nationwide training for churches to begin ministries to international students, are provided. Students from many lands and religions are attracted to the mission. Served in the spirit of the Good Samaritan, each student who comes for help, whatever his or her nationality or faith may be, is welcomed with love.

As reported in the September/October 1997 copy of *The Real Issue* (83), a somewhat similar program operates off the campus of the University of Minnesota in the home of and under the leadership of Kathleen and Chris Macosko, both of whom serve full-time at the university. Others of the community who share the Macosko's love and concern for those from abroad studying in a strange land assist them. Like Tom and Liz Stewart, Kathleen and Chris Macosko welcome and serve all who come—whatever their faiths may be—in a spirit of love.

I close this chapter with a statement by President Thomas Jefferson, a portion of a National Prayer for Peace presented by him on the occasion of his Second Inaugural as reported in William J. Federer's *America's God and Country Encyclopedia of Quotations* (84):

> Almighty God, Who has given us this good land for our heritage; We humbly beseech Thee that we may always prove ourselves a people mindful of Thy favor and glad to do Thy will. Bless our land with honorable ministry, sound learning, and pure manners.

> Save us from violence, discord, and confusion, from pride and arrogance, and from every evil way. Defend our liberties, and fashion into one united people the multitude brought hither out of many kindreds and tongues (85).

Chapter VI

Coping with America's Moral and Spiritual Decline

As indicated in earlier chapters, I believe the two most powerful contributors in the shaping of the lives of individuals and nations are <u>education</u> and <u>religion</u>. Before proceeding further, let me review "from where I come" in relation to each of the two.

<u>I am an educator</u>. More specifically, I have been involved as a student, teacher, researcher, counselor, and/or administrator in American public education for nearly all of my life. I am a product of America's public education system; and I am most grateful for the quality, relevant educational opportunities that have been mine.

With deep appreciation to private and parochial educational institutions in America for their significant contributions to the development of our nation and its people especially in the early life of America, it is public education with its service to the masses to which much credit must be given. The genius of American public education has been, and continues to be, its relevance to our nation's needs and its availability to all of our citizens—people of all talents, of all levels of ability, and of all religious faiths.

The opportunities to study and to learn in public education institutions, preschool through doctoral study, together with the privileges that have been mine to serve in public education institutions during most of my professional life, have led to my enthusiasm for and my pride in public education. In my various international involvements I have not observed any educational programs as meaningful and as relevant in the service of people as is public education in the USA. Yes, there are those from elitist educational systems in other nations that, in the comparing of test results of their selected few with those of the masses of graduates of a much broader ability range from American higher education institutions, have taken pride in their superiority. Even some of our own citizens, without considering the lack of comparability of some of the data, observe that American education is not doing well, all the while overlooking the real genius of our comprehensive education program <u>in serving all students to the extent that each can benefit</u> and in dignifying all worthwhile labor done well.

With regard to my religious beliefs, having been born into a Christian home and nurtured by the Christian faith all of my life, I believe in God—Father, Son, and Holy Spirit <u>as one</u>, not as three. As God among us, Jesus taught us that living in love of God and of each other <u>is the essence of the Christian faith</u>. And in the realization of the Holy Spirit at work within us and among us, we can experience God's Kingdom "on earth, as it is in heaven."

My faith provides not only for my own spiritual nurture and the formation of the mind and life of Christ within me, but also for my acceptance of all peoples of the world as friends and neighbors. My Christian faith leads me to embrace and welcome those from other lands and faiths to the United States of America, which, although founded in the Judeo-Christian tradition, welcomes each of its citizens to the opportunity to worship as he or she chooses.

Through the years, I have been privileged to work with and to come to love those of many faiths other than my own. There is much we have in common, and we need to join together in love and trust to reverse America's moral and spiritual decline.

America has no "national religion" for as already noted, those who founded our nation made clear in the First Amendment of the United States Constitution that the government shall not prescribe any one religious faith for its citizens. They also established the historical fact that America is a nation "under God." The words and the pronouncements of this nation's Founders, including John Adams, Samuel Adams, George Washington, Benjamin Franklin, Alexander Hamilton, Patrick Henry, and Thomas Jefferson, as presented in *One Nation Under God* (21), and as shared earlier in this volume, attest to the fact that our nation was indeed founded on spiritual bases.

Some American citizens observe that there is a contradiction at this point, and object to any mention of America's spiritual undergirdings, even though such has been established historically. I would note, however, that American citizens who have come from other lands and faiths have declared their allegiance to their adopted nation founded "under God," and are grateful for their many opportunities in America, especially the freedom to worship as they wish.

Some critics choose to ignore the second part of the First Amendment. They support the first portion that states, "Congress shall make no law respecting an establishment of religion," but they minimize or ignore the second that assures all Americans "the free exercise of religion." All of which brings me to the matter of prayer—especially prayer in public education institutions.

I believe in prayer. It is through prayer that we nurture the spirit. It is through prayer that we come to know God—to love God—to serve God—and to honor God. It has been encouraging to observe how many people, some who appear not to be especially religious, in certain circumstances and under certain conditions, turn to prayer. Someone has observed that "as long as there are final examinations, there will be prayers in schools!"

In times of crisis, most of us (if at a point where we can no longer handle our problems alone) will turn to prayer for help and understanding. The great numbers of prayer chains active in support of those who are ill, are grieving, or are experiencing tragedy of one kind or another, attest to the belief of many, including medical doctors, in the value of prayer. In my own experience, as a seven-year-old boy, a younger brother was near death with a severe case of pneumonia. As our family doctor was leaving our home after a visit, he observed, "I've done all I can. Only prayer can save him now." Members of the immediate family—uncles, aunts, cousins—and some loving friends and neighbors who had gathered did pray. And there was recovery.

It is encouraging that, as mentioned earlier, most Americans continue to look to God at the most significant times and moments in their lives. Prayers are offered at the bar mitzvah of young people of Jewish faith and at the christening and baptism of children of Christian faith, at the marriages of sons and daughters, and at the burial of loved ones even though some of the people involved may not manifest the same measure of spirituality on other occasions of life. Certainly, prayers are needed as we deal with America's decline in its moral and spiritual values.

When we consider the role of religion in our public educational institutions, it is generally agreed that we do not want government or other outside agencies to prescribe prayers or other religious expressions in our public schools. And we do not want to infringe upon the rights of peoples of all faiths to manifest them in a free America, including in its public schools. We need freedom of expression of our differing faiths in our educational institutions both to give support to the religious teachings of homes and churches in the total development of individual students and to provide general education experiences for each other in achieving understanding of the religions of our friends and neighbors of the world.

Again, I would point out that I oppose government-prescribed prayers for public schools—or, for that matter, any prayers <u>designated for all students</u>. I do however, support periods of silence in which each student may pray as he or she chooses. These occasions could be on a regular basis, as well as on special occasions. Such would emphasize the importance of prayer without offense to those of differing faiths.

What about prayer on public occasions? I believe each of us, whatever our faith may be, if asked to pray in public, should pray in the fullest tradition of our respective faith without a "watering down" of our prayers. However, out of respect and consideration of those of different faiths, each should share in the offering of prayers on public occasions rather than those of one or two faiths praying always for a group made up of those of several faiths.

In our nation's Pledge of Allegiance we (all USA citizens, whatever our religious faiths may be) do acknowledge America as "one nation under God." Such appropriately recognizes that although people of many different faiths choose to come to America to live, to work, and to rear their families, the founding bases in establishing our great democracy were <u>in the Judeo-Christian tradition—and must continue in such</u> if America is to remain true to its heritage.

As mentioned frequently in this volume, peoples of all faiths are welcome in America and are free to worship as they believe. But this does not alter the single most important element in the establishment of the USA as the greatest democratic nation ever founded—namely that <u>we are "a nation under God."</u> The foundation of America was profoundly religious. It is appropriate that today the various affairs of America's governmental bodies at all levels and in their various activities acknowledge God and pray to Him for guidance.

It is appropriate also that the various military services of the USA continue to provide for the spiritual needs of those who serve their country. Like America, our Armed Services are becoming more pluralistic. The same measure of individualized spiritual guidance and comfort that has been available to military personnel in America's traditional faiths—Catholic, Jewish, and Protestant—must, of course, be available for those of all faiths who are serving our nation and its citizens.

Finally, I would underscore that prayer can have its greatest meaning when done privately. Jesus observed:

> And when thou prayest, thou shalt not be as the
> hypocrites are: for they love to pray standing in the

synagogues and in the corners of the streets, that they may be seen of men. Verily I say unto you, They have their reward. But thou, when thou prayest, enter into thy closet, and when thou hast shut thy door, pray to thy Father which is in secret; and thy Father which seeth in secret shall reward thee openly (Matthew 6:5-6).

In considering how best to cope with our nation's decline in its moral and spiritual values, I repeat that I come as a life-long public education teacher and administrator who believes that education and religion are essential influences in the shaping of people and of nations; and that in their coming together rests our best hope and assurance of reversing our nation's current decline in its values.

I repeat again that homes and churches must regain their roles as the <u>primary</u> lead agencies of society in the teaching and the strengthening of the values of the young people of America. At the same time, however, the realities of the current lessened influence of both homes and churches in accomplishing this mission lead me to propose a <u>greater involvement for public education in values training</u>—that being primarily <u>one of strong support of homes and churches of different faiths in their rightful lead roles</u>. For those students who have shared in home and church emphases on moral and spiritual values, there is need for <u>reinforcement</u> of those learnings in their public schools experiences. For those who have had little or no orientation to moral and spiritual values in their homes or churches, there is need for considerable values orientation and emphasis.

There are steps within the law that public education institutions can take to help fill the tragic values void possessed by so many young people today—a void, which if not filled, will certainly lead to a worsening of the current decline in our nation's values, and could lead to the demise of our nation! Chapters VII and VIII offer suggestions of what public education institutions can do to supplement homes and churches in achieving <u>the best of</u>

mind and spirit.

Before considering, additionally, what we as the people of America may do to reverse our nation's current decline in its moral and spiritual values, let us reflect once again on the basic elements in the founding of our great democracy—Judeo-Christian values; the subsequent establishment of laws based on responsibility; and a form of government that when coupled with abundant natural resources gave promise of greatness for the new nation and its people for centuries to come.

We need to think seriously about the original undergirding of the fledgling nation, a foundation that today is deteriorating, as our present values decline suggests. We need to recall and to study once again the words and the actions of our Founders. Most basic of all considerations (and the cornerstone in the establishment of the foundation for the new nation) is belief and trust in a living God—an Almighty God of love, justice, and righteousness. Thomas Jefferson, primary drafter of the Declaration of Independence, America's third President, a noted author, educator, architect, and scientist, who founded the University of Virginia, in his "Notes on the State of Virginia" (86), made this statement as quoted in *One Nation Under God* (21):

> God who gave us life gave us liberty. And can the liberties of a nation be thought secure when we have removed their only firm basis, a conviction in the minds of the people that these liberties are of the gift of God? That they are not to be violated but with His wrath? Indeed, I tremble for my country when I reflect that God is just; that His justice cannot sleep forever (21), (p. 30).

To be sure, there are evidences that we continue in various ways and to varying degrees as a nation "under God," as stated in our Pledge of Allegiance to the flag of the USA. Our coins continue to bear the engraving, "In God We Trust." Our public officials at all levels of governance, in the taking of their respective oaths of office, place their hands on the Bible and affirm their commitment to God. Chaplains pray to God for guidance of the members of the United States Senate and the House of Representatives, as they do also for state legislative leaders. Additionally, chaplains serve those in the various USA military programs.

The above, together with other examples that might be stated, indicate that the God of our Founders continues to a considerable extent as Lord of our nation even in the face of the opposition of some of our fellow citizens. Certainly, the most insidious contributor to our problems today and the primary cause of the widest cracks in the founding structure of America is the "turning of their backs" to God by many, whether expressed through outright statements of disbelief or through the all-too-prevalent lukewarm "nod of the head" posture in relation to Him by so many of us.

In the generally good times in which we live, there are some who do not sense the need for God. And in view of the vastness of our technological developments and the explosive growth of our body of knowledge, we have become somewhat as gods ourselves. So why bother about the Supreme Being we call God? Yes, it is good—and still fashionable—to look to God and to call on Him on the occasions of our weddings, the christening or bar mitzvahing of our children, and the burial of our loved ones, as mentioned earlier. Many however, really do not sense the need for God in life generally. Is it any wonder the foundation of the spiritually guided form of democracy that is our nation's great heritage is destructing?

Have we possibly in these good times and comforts contributed to our nation's decline in its values by ignoring the need to assume certain responsibilities essential to preserving the good life? Have we been all too willing to accommodate, without question, some points of view and behaviors that have been and are contrary to the thoughts and actions at the heart of our nation's founding? I think so. Permit me to elaborate before continuing with proposals of some steps to be taken, which could help to get our nation back on track again.

First and foremost, we need to recognize that the basic values of our nation are to be understood essentially as originally intended at the time of its founding. They are not to be changed for our own convenience to serve the needs of varying circumstances. A serious threat to the survival of our nation comes from those who would alter the history of our founding. We must deal with this threat, acting with high commitment and deep faith, as we dialogue with those who argue for a substantial overhaul of the USA Constitution, who believe in and promote America's "New Morality," who oppose any mention of God in public life including in our public schools, who contend that in the name of freedom they may say and do whatever they wish regardless of how despicable their words or actions may be and what other citizens desire. Every American citizen born in this land (along with all from other lands who choose to become American citizens) should gratefully acknowledge this nation's spiritual undergirding, for it is out of such and because of such that there was formed the greatest democratic nation in history! We must not alter the two significant facts: that we were founded as a nation under God, and that we are free to worship as we please. The first is a historical fact. The second, also a historical fact, was an action by the very same Founders of our nation, who made it clear in the First Amendment that all USA citizens are free to worship as they choose. Additionally, it should be noted that we have prospered abundantly as a nation under God and that our greatest hope in coping with present problems rests in returning to the spiritual beliefs and commitments that were basic in our founding—those immutable beliefs and values which, if followed, will assure continued greatness of the United States of America. We must, as Jesus taught:

> Seek ye first the Kingdom of God, and his right-eousness; and all these things shall be added unto you (Matthew 6:33).

Moving on to Chapter VII, let us consider some suggestions of steps to be taken by our nation in coping with its values decline, with special attention to the key role of public education in the process. Although some of the proposals may at first glance appear elementary, they are <u>foundational</u> and could prove to be profound in efforts to reverse our nation's decline in its moral and spiritual values.

Chapter VII

Broad Proposals
of What May Be Done

As shared previously, I am a product of public education and have been an advocate of it all of my professional life. Also, in concluding Chapter VI, in which I indicated "from where I come" both educationally and spiritually, I underscored the need for public education to become more involved than is currently the case in supporting the development of the moral and spiritual values of students.

Although many agencies of society (especially homes and churches, but also others, such as the various media, our courts, and the entertainment industry) must be involved in a common effort to reclaim for America its former high level of moral and spiritual values, it is public education, with its capacity to reach the masses of young people (building upon its already well-established academic base) that must step forward at this time with some bold, courageous initiatives to augment academic learnings with clearly understood and stated values emphases. To be sure, many of these emphases should be of a supportive nature to the primary values initiatives of homes and churches. All, however, should be parts of the larger society's shared efforts to reverse our nation's present values decline.

As noted in Chapter III, some academic programs (especially in the sciences and technology, due in part to considerable research emphasis and substantial funding) have progressed beyond the understandings and abilities of many people to manage them wisely. Some, including distinguished scientists, have warned that knowledge without benefit of moral and spiritual guidance in its use can lead to destruction. Jesus reminded us that "man shall not live by bread alone, but by every word that proceedeth out of the mouth of God" (Matthew 4:4).

A lifetime of involvement in education leads me to believe that public education, at this time, is in the strongest and most advantageous position of all agencies of society to bring concerned individuals and groups together in a shared effort to improve the level of America's moral and spiritual behavior. Accordingly, I have elected to discuss early in this chapter the essential role of public education in values training, recognizing the continuing need for homes and churches once again to become the lead agencies in this effort.

Before calling on those outside of public education to join with education in a coordinated effort to reverse our present values decline, I must acknowledge that my public education colleagues and I have not done as well as we should have in helping our students achieve the wisdom essential to guide them in the use of all that they know. All too often we have stood by and permitted a takeover of public education by secular interests, abdicating our leadership and abandoning the foresight and wisdom of those who founded our nation and those who guided our schools prior to recent decades. Now, however, there appear to be indications of an increased awareness of the extent of our nation's values problems as well as of the various contributing factors. We are awakening once again to the need for public education to assume greater responsibilities in the total education of students, including values education.

We in public education currently have the opportunity working with other concerned agencies, to play a major role in healing the present values malaise in America. We must not let this opportunity pass. We are perilously close to the time when recovery may be beyond our abilities to affect.

Reference was made in Chapter IV of this volume of some current efforts to enhance the quality of American higher education by the National Association of State Universities and Land-Grant Colleges and the American Council on Education. Each has singled out for special attention the needs for both academic improvements and for greater attention to student values.

The NASULGC position, as stated in *Returning to Our Roots— The Student Experience* (3) was shared in Chapter IV, and bears repeating:

> Values deserve special attention in this effort. The biggest educational challenge we face revolves around developing character, conscience, citizenship, tolerance, civility, and individual and social responsibility in our students. We must not ignore this obligation in a society that sometimes gives the impression that virtues such as these are discretionary. These should be standard equipment, not options, in our graduates (3).

Concurrent with the efforts of the NASULGC has been the American Council on Education's preparation of a special issue of its magazine *Educational Record*, devoted entirely to the subject of "College and Character: Preparing Students for Lives of Civic Responsibility" (5). Stanley O. Ikenberry, ACE President, in his introductory statement entitled, "Values, Character, Leadership: Reexamining our Mission," made a number of observations reported in Chapter IV, including the following:

> For whatever combination of reasons, a broader public agenda that is concerned with values, civic life, the common good, and related questions is challenging us to think more carefully about higher education's ultimate purposes. It is about time, after half a century of focusing on campus growth, specialized professions, and the transmission of information, for higher education to broaden the discus-

sion to include some of the intangible, more difficult to define qualities of what it means to be an "educated person." In part, the demand for this may be driven by the decline in the quality of civic life in the larger society and by a concern that colleges can and should do something about it (5).

I would repeat also at this time that in another ACE publication of a half century ago entitled *The Student Personnel Point of View* (4), it was stated:

> The concept of education is broadened to include attention to the student's well-rounded development—<u>physically, socially, emotionally and spiritually, as well as intellectually</u>.

I am encouraged by the observations and efforts of both the National Association of State Universities and Land-Grant Colleges and the American Council on Education. Appreciation is expressed to the leadership of both of these prestigious national higher education associations, as well as to their colleagues who have been active and/or continue to be involved in the NASULGC and ACE projects. And appreciation is due also to the leadership of the American Council on Education of a half century ago in recognizing the importance of the spiritual dimension in the total educational development of students.

As I have noted previously, it is my belief that the two most powerful entities in the shaping of the lives of both individuals and of nations are education and religion. I am encouraged, especially, that the ACE acknowledged the high role of religion in both its 1949 and its 1997 statements. The 1997 ACE publication (5) included a chapter entitled, "Religious Faith and the Development of Character on Campus" (14), written by William H. Willimon, dean of the chapel and professor of Christian Ministry at Duke University. Some of his thoughts will be presented in Chapter VIII.

Before discussing additionally the essential spiritual role in values education, I would acknowledge the attention of some public colleges and universities (as well as some public schools) to values education, although with little or no reference to any religious roots or associations. Actually, some of the values emphasized in secular education do stem from traditional religious teachings, while others are creations of the present, designed by individuals or groups of varied backgrounds, experiences, and understandings of how to serve present needs. "Situational Ethics" is an example of the latter, with decisions of what is right or wrong based largely on what best serves the needs of the moment. Generally lacking are any references to such time-proven, unchanging "guidelines" as the Golden Rule and the Ten Commandments. A recent encouraging exception was made in a July 8, 1998 statement by Oklahoma's State Superintendent of Public Instruction, Sandy Garrett, in which she referred to "the Holy Bible as a great teaching source for morality" (87). As reported in the lead editorial of the July 22, 1998 issue of *The Daily Oklahoman*, she stated:

> We can't assume that students believe you shouldn't kill people, you shouldn't steal or cheat, you should honor your parents and respect the laws of the land. These are the simple truths we hold self-evident and they are the truths we can reinforce in class through the study of great literary works by Aristotle, Shakespeare, Madison and Lincoln and those included in the Holy Bible.

State Superintendent Garrett also has used other means, both statewide and nationally, to convey her commitment to character and values education, such as her periodic addresses to Oklahoma educators.

In the summer 1997 issue of the Delta Kappa Gamma *Bulletin* is a commendable article written by the husband-wife team of public schools educators, David and Ruth Ann Wilson, entitled, "Teaching Positive Values in the Classroom" (88). They noted:

> Character education—the transmitting of values to

students—is an inescapable, inherent part of a teacher's job and one that should be actively embraced.

The authors continue by listing four sound arguments why teachers should be enthusiastic proponents for character education. First, "positive values lead to positive outcomes." Six positive values are then listed: honesty, responsibility, hard work, helpfulness, respect for others, and fairness. Second, the classroom is an extension of society. Third, school may be the primary source of instruction on positive values for some children. And, fourth, classroom instruction and values go hand and hand.

There are many other resources noting the problem and guiding us in values education at different levels. In this volume reference has been made previously to *The Soul of the American University: From Protestant Establishment to Established Nonbelief* (15), authored by George Marsden. Also, I would mention *The Challenge of Pluralism: Education, Politics, and Values* (89), Power R. Clark and Daniel Lapsley, editors, 1992.

In a recent issue of *The Christian Science Monitor*, Sara Terry Gabrels wrote an article entitled, "The Age of Casting No Stones" (90). She noted:

> They come into Thomas Donaldson's classroom eager to learn about ethics—young freshmen, he says, "ready to defend their values, almost idealistically so." But, he adds, for all their convictions about ethical behavior, these students also say, "Whatever anybody else thinks of ethics is right for them."
>
> Mr. Donaldson, who directs the ethics program at the Wharton School of the University of Pennsylvania, lauds the fact there's an underlying defense of tolerance and pluralism in the student's comments. But he's concerned that there's something crucial missing in their reasoning and ability to make broader determinations about right and wrong

(90).

She also observed:

> Ethicists agree that the reestablishment of a moral
> center is not likely to come through politicians or at
> a national level. Discussion, they say, must take place
> in communities—in groups like families, churches,
> and businesses.

In 1959, I was asked by the editor of *Faculty Forum* (91), published by the Division of Educational Institutions of The Methodist Church and the Board of Christian Education of the Presbyterian Church, U.S., to review a book entitled *The College Influence on Student Character* (92), by Dr. Edward D. Eddy, who defined character as "intelligent direction and purposeful control of conduct by definite moral principles" (92), (p. 2).

Over a one-year period Eddy and two assistants went to the campuses of 20 American colleges and universities and visited with "several thousands" of students. The methodology (especially at the time) was unique in that each student "spoke his or her mind." The book reflected <u>what students think</u> rather than what a writer might observe to be the thinking of students. Among other things, students made it clear that for the teacher to concern himself or herself with subject matter alone is not enough—that the teacher has a responsibility to see that students are encouraged to develop character attributes that will serve them well. One student commented that one of his instructors, "in his teaching, and just in his very being has given my life more purpose and direction than any other person I know."

In the February 10, 1998 issue of *The Christian Science Monitor* (93) was a splendid article by Thomas H. Groome, a professor of theology and education at Boston College and author of *Educating for Life: A Spiritual Vision for Every Teacher and Parent* (94). In *The Christian Science Monitor* article (93), entitled " . . . And Infuse Education with More Spiritual Values," the writer noted that "neither money nor technology will cure the present ills of education in America." Groome also noted that there are spiritual values on which many of the great world religions and spiritualities reach consensus (94).

We certainly should commend the efforts of the many excellent teachers, counselors, and other public schools personnel who recognize the need for values education concurrent with academic learnings and who try to provide such, albeit in a climate that generally frowns on mention of the spiritual dimension. The facts are, however, that without acknowledging the need for moral and spiritual foundations—without attention to spiritual absolutes, such as "Thou shall not kill" (your fellow students, or anyone else!)—without the learning of time-proven values which guide us in life's varying situations, our essentially secular efforts to lead in values education are not going to get the job done!

William J. Bennett (formerly United States Secretary of Education) in an article published in *IMPRIMIS*,[d] (based on an address he made on the occasion of The Heritage Foundation's 20th anniversary) spoke on the subject of "Revolt Against God—America's Spiritual Despair" (95). He noted that "the real crisis of our time is spiritual." Following is an excerpt from his address:

> We desperately need to recover a sense of the fundamental purpose of education, which is to provide for the intellectual and moral education of the young.
>
> As individuals and as a society, we need to return religion to its proper place. Religion, after all, provides us with moral bearings. And if I am right and the chief problem we face is spiritual impoverishment, then the solution depends, finally, on spiritual renewal. I am not speaking here about coerced spiritual renewal—in fact, there is no such thing—but about renewal freely taken (95).

What can—and must—public education do? As already mentioned, public education can do some things directly; and, in other situations, education should be primarily in supportive roles.

My first proposal is that public education, in addition to recognizing the many good things about our great land must come to know and to acknowledge the seriousness of America's current decline in its moral and spiritual values. We in education need to face up to the fact that all is not well in our nation, nor in our public schools. We need to recognize that there has been a lessening of the influence of both homes and churches in their traditional lead roles of providing values education and that public education institutions must, in a number of ways, pick up the slack.

It follows then that a second proposal be that public schools, working largely in a supportive role with homes and churches, must become more involved in values education concurrent with academic learnings. Certainly, as reported earlier, the calls for action from the leadership of both the American Council on Education and of the National Association of State Universities and Land-Grant Colleges as well as from other individuals and organizations concerned with America's values crisis are both timely and appreciated!

A third proposal is that we in public education urge each student to be active in the church of his or her choice. Such a stance by public education would say to students who have not had values education in their homes or in their churches that spiritual nurture and development are important elements of becoming fully educated. For those students who have had values education in their homes and churches, such an emphasis by public school teachers, administrators, and other staff would communicate to them that public education emphasizes the need for religion in one's total development. Such supportive efforts by public education could, in the long run, be the single most important step to be taken in restoring America's moral and spiritual values!

Another way to communicate an institution's commitment to and support of religion would be to reinstate and support a program popular on public education campuses in earlier years—an

95

annual religious emphasis period to supplement the institution's announced support of the religious element in one's education. The leadership of all faith groups wishing to participate would be asked to select one or more speakers from on and off-campus to minister to their own faith group as well as to serve in a general education role in orienting those of other faiths who wish to learn more about the spiritual beliefs of their fellow students.

A REW program (Religious Emphasis Week) should not be established to proselytize, but rather to underscore for those of all faiths the importance of the spiritual dimension in the total educational experience. For many students, such an event might well be the first opportunity for them to be introduced to religion and its high role in our lives.

It is interesting to note at this point that while we in America are experiencing a decline in the role of religion in our lives as some among us actively seek ways to divorce our nation and its people from our spiritual roots that many from nations around the world are welcoming the presence of religion in rebuilding their nations "under God" as did our Founders. Included are some newly-freed from anti-religion, communist control.

To those who argue against the proposal just made, I would once again note that public education may not become a pulpit for any one religion, but that all of us in America have the right to believe and to worship as we wish. I repeat that I do not propose that public education institutions take over the responsibilities of homes and churches in spiritual values education, but that public education be supportive, strongly supportive, of homes and churches in their acknowledged lead roles in values education by communicating its own high commitment to both academic and spiritual growth as the two essential components in becoming fully educated—in achieving the best of both mind and spirit.

We, as a nation, must turn once again to God, our Creator and Sustainer—the God of all history, including the founding of America and of other nations. Disbelief offers very little of substance and hope to humankind in our quest to achieve dignity and the best of which we, individually and collectively, are created to be and can become.

A fourth proposal relates to the need for leadership. From where must the leadership come in bringing public education to the position of acknowledging, and pronouncing, (without apology and reservation) that emphases on both education and religion are essential in the total development of students? It must, first and foremost, come from those locally—public school superintendents and principals, college and university presidents and deans, school boards, governing bodies, teachers, counselors, residence halls staff, athletic coaches, and other staff. Certainly, the job to be done is not one for government—nationally or at the state level—to mandate. It is a responsibility of local educators, working closely with local homes and churches (although I would hope, with the support and encouragement of educational colleagues and organizations regionally and nationally).

I would especially underscore the need for leadership by administrators in public education—public school superintendents and principals, college and university presidents, deans, and department heads. It is they who set the tone of educational communities, whether in encouraging students to attend the churches of their choice or in assuring a "free marketplace" for all religious faiths at the institutions which they serve. It is they who must also lead in resolving the host of other issues, needs, and responsibilities confronting educators today, including the assuring of excellence in teaching, research, public service, and outreach. It is they, if committed to the best of both mind and spirit and leading their respective institutions accordingly, who will be the prime movers in reversing America's current decline in moral and spiritual values.

In 1972, James MacGregor Burns wrote a Pulitzer Prize and National Book Award-winning book entitled *Leadership* (96)—a volume which has meant much to me in my continuing education and service in higher education. In his "Prologue: The Crisis of Leadership," he has observed:

. . . *moral leadership* concerns me the most. By this term I mean, first, that leaders and led have a relationship not only of power but of mutual needs, aspirations, and values; second, that in responding to leaders, followers have adequate knowledge of alternative leaders and programs and the capacity to choose among those alternatives; and, third, that leaders take responsibility for their commitments— if they promise certain kinds of economic, social, and political change, they assume leadership in the bringing about of that change. Moral leadership is not mere preaching, or the uttering of pieties, or the insistence on social conformity. Moral leadership emerges from, and always returns to, the fundamental wants and needs, aspirations, and values of the followers (96), (p. 4).

In 1982, I wrote a book entitled *Leadership for Leadership, Number One Priority for Presidents and Other Administrators* (97)—the primary emphasis being that the <u>highest and best in leadership is in the leading of others to become leaders</u>.(q) Among other matters, I spoke of "shared governance" (without abdication, however, by presidents [and others of defined administrative duties] of their ultimate decision-making responsibilities). Also, I spoke of the moral and spiritual aspects of leadership (97), (pp. 97-103).

I would mention one other essential dimension of leadership at this time, that being <u>effective communications</u>. If public education is to fulfill its responsibilities in a shared effort with homes, churches, and other agencies of society in restoring a high level of moral and spiritual values in America, there must be effective communications among those who lead, as well as among all others who share and serve in the monumental task before us.

As part of this discussion of leadership, let me comment on a relatively new tool—the Internet—now being utilized by Christian Leadership Ministries. Keith Seabourn, Director of Internet Development, in a CLM publication, May 12, 1998, entitled *Telling the Truth on the Internet: A "How To" Guide* (98), noted that this 24-hours-per-day vehicle for a world-wide ministry has come at a time when many are critical of the Internet for its sharing of much that is negative and undesirable. CLM, however, views the Internet as "God's latest gift to the church"—a means of mass communication that is far cheaper than any other means and which reaches all over the world in ways that no other technology can.

Seabourn added:

> The early church expanded and flourished in a hostile culture because they saw the importance of sending bold, thoughtful, trained apologists to take the gospel into new and varied cultures. The pathway that enabled the rapid expansion of the gospel was the Roman highway system. Today, we have a new Roman Road . . . the worldwide electronic computer communication network known as the Internet. Today, the church needs to return to sending bold, thoughtful, trained apologists worldwide, now using the Internet communication system (98).

One of today's "bold, thoughtful, trained apologists" (using Seabourn's term) is Frederica Mathewes-Green who, in the September/October 1998 issue of *The Real Issue*, commented that "Character Does Matter" (99). She is a commentator for the Odyssey Network (*News Odyssey*) and a *Christianity Today* columnist. In Chapter II of this volume, she was quoted from her article in the January 12, 1998 issue of *Christianity Today*, entitled "Wanted: A New Pro-Life Strategy" (45). Additional comments by her on that subject also appear in Chapter IX of this book.

The "Character Does Matter" article is a transcript of a lecture to faculty presented at the University of Delaware's annual leadership breakfast, co-sponsored by Christian Leadership Ministries of Campus Crusade for Christ. Mathewes-Green acknowledges quickly that leadership can be both for good and for evil and "Leadership without Character is Hell." Selected quotes from her "Character Does Matter" presentation follow:[h]

> Everyone is born with a rudimentary conscience, but it gets formed and affected by the culture we live in . . . . The essential thing everyone needs is self-esteem. . . . But I'm saying that self-esteem is no guarantor of good behavior; in fact, it can merely confirm a person in bad behavior.

> I'm recommending something more like the opposite of self-esteem. I'm recommending that you question yourself and your presuppositions—that you practice humility and modesty, and be ready to admit that you could be wrong; that you be especially wary of the ways your culture has shaped your conscience.

The author of "Character Does Matter" (99) continued with discussion of "Principles to Live By." She noted:

> So if we can't live without character, and if we can't trust what we automatically find inside as a good guide, how can we know what principles to live by?

> I think we have to look beyond current fashion, and seek out the values that are timeless, the elements of justice and moral behavior that have been upheld by the broadest range of humans across cultures, throughout time, and around the world.

> Try this: "Love your enemies, do good to those who hate you, bless those who curse you, pray for those who abuse you." Frankly, this is very bad advice—if your only goal is being a successful leader. It's not in the management books. But being a big worldly success, with a corner office and a title on the door, is apparently not Jesus' aim. You can't be that impressive a leader, you know, if your community ends up

by nailing you to a tree.

Did Jesus teach that good leadership required good character? Jesus turned the sequence upside down. It seems that being effective—being a competent, powerful, efficient and acknowledged leader—isn't as important to Him as doing the right, just, good, and noble thing—acting with character.

As Mother Teresa said when people pointed out to her the futility of rescuing the dying from Calcutta's slums, God doesn't call us to be successful, He calls us to be faithful.

Those who follow Christ will find their whole worldview is transformed. Like Mother Teresa, you will look for the path of faithfulness, of upright character, over the path of easy success. You will hunger for deeper transformation inside, so that its not just your outside deeds that are superficially correct. You'll discover an ever-increasing desire to be changed from deep within, and to be saved from the hell that we make for ourselves and each other by our daily, petty, stupid sins and selfishness.

When you are transformed like this, you find that you are becoming an entirely different sort of leader. The light that spills out of you will illuminate those around you and change their lives. It is not a leadership of power, but one of service. It is subversive. It is unconquerable. And it is impossible to lose anything because you have already given it all away.

May you respond to the call of Jesus Christ to be that kind of transformed soul. May you live in that love night and day (99).

A fifth proposal—one closely intertwined with the others previously presented—is that of assuring in all of public education at all levels and for students of all differing religious backgrounds, a "free marketplace," where all students feel welcome and where all are encouraged to manifest fully their respective religious faiths. As already acknowledged, public education institutions may not establish any one church to serve students generally or to serve any one faith group only. But public education can and must make clear to those of all faith groups that all are welcome, and all are encouraged to live and to manifest fully their respective religious beliefs. Of course we must also demonstrate by both what we do and say that all of different faiths (including faculty and staff) are accepted and appreciated, are free to worship in accordance with their respective faiths, and have the right to speak freely in relation to the religious faith that is most meaningful to each of them—as I have done in the writing of *The Best of Mind and Spirit*.

Certainly, there should be communication between and among those of different faiths. The free marketplace allows for dialogue—for exciting, supplementary educational experiences in coming to know friends and neighbors from other nations, cultures, and religions. We have in common many beliefs and values. These need to be shared and understood if we are to live together in love, trust, and goodwill.

I am aware that in a free marketplace some believe they are at liberty to say and to do as they please without respect for others. I would repeat that we are free only within a framework of love and respect for the rights and the welfare of others.

Related to the preceding, and presented as a sixth proposal of what may be done in under-girding the spiritual aspect of students' total educational experiences, I propose that public higher education institutions consider establishing a department of religious studies at the undergraduate level. Some institutions may wish to provide graduate level study, such as is offered by the University of Iowa in its highly regarded School of Religion. The present proposal, however, is for undergraduate, elective courses only, regarding the spiritual faiths of the world's peoples, to be taught by well-qualified representatives of the different faiths. Courses should be offered for the purpose of acquainting interested students with the different religions of the world, but not for the purpose of proselytizing.

In a religious studies program every effort should be made to present the distinctiveness and the full thrust of each religion studied. The seeking of common denominators among different faiths is helpful, although if considered instead of or apart from a full study of each religion, it can lead to a diluted presentation of individual faiths.

I would note at this point, that the first fully-endowed professorship at the university with which I have been associated for more than four decades was in religious studies. This, to some degree, has communicated to the academic community that the study of religion is an important component of the total educational experience on the campus.

Before departing from this discussion about the teaching of courses in religion I share the following comments by Kenneth I. Brown, former president of Hiram College and of Denison University, from his book *Not Minds Alone* (16). He observed:

> A department of religion demands the highest level of scholarly competence. It must be taught by men (sic) whose preparation is equal of the best members of the faculty. It asks no favors; it seeks no exceptions from departmental regulations. It is content to stand on its own feet (16), (p. 143).

Finally, as we contemplate the massive task of reversing America's current decline in its moral and spiritual values, it should be recognized that the process of regaining a higher values level in our nation will take time. Some efforts, I would hope, will lead to early favorable results. Despite our best efforts, however, most of what we do initially will result in modest changes. There is need, first of all, to stem present trends. Only after such is accomplished, can an actual reversal of the present situation begin. Years, even decades, of insensitivity to what was happening to our nation's values have brought us to our present crisis. Considerable commitment, resolve, and effort by those directly involved in reversing our values decline, together with the dedicated support of our nation's citizenry, will be needed to get the job done. And borrowing from a statement by Benjamin Franklin (26), (pp. 23, 24), we must seek God's guidance and help. We are told in the book of The Proverbs in the Old Testament of the Bible:

> Trust in the Lord with all thine heart; and lean not unto thine own understanding. In all thy ways acknowledge Him, and He shall direct thy paths (Proverbs 3:5-6).

Whether an individual or a nation is in crisis, the words of Franklin and of the writer of Proverbs are so relevant! <u>We must look to God for healing and restoration</u>.

John Newton's hymn entitled "Amazing Grace" (written at a time of great crisis in Newton's life) has much meaning for America and its citizens at this time of its moral and spiritual crisis. Judy Collins, singer and writer, in the introduction to her publication entitled *Amazing Grace* (100) observed:

> "Amazing Grace" has had a profound effect on many singers. Joan Baez, Jessye Norman, Arlo Guthrie, Arethra Franklin, Sam Cooke; every singer who knows a good melody and a great lyric has sung it at some time. Its sweet directness goes straight to the heart (100), (p. 8).

In addition, the author noted:

> "Amazing Grace" transcends religions, cultures, color, geography. People all over the world sing it, as a prayer, as a consolation, as a jewel of great beauty, and a hope in a world torn with strife. It is the pearl of spiritual songs, produced in the face of sin and

desolation and offering hope to each soul who is touched by its profound message (100), (p. 9).

As a seventh proposal—one which may take some time to impact the values crisis—I propose that college and university teacher-education departments provide for their students who are preparing to teach, to counsel, and to serve young people subsequently, an orientation to our nation's values crisis, and its implications in terms of what is happening to America. The uniquely significant roles teachers, counselors, advisers, coaches, and others who work especially closely with students can have in reversing the present decline in America's moral and spiritual values needs to be emphasized. Chapter VIII is devoted largely to the what and the how of realizing the full potential of those who work closest with students in their day to day efforts to encourage and to underscore the best of both mind and spirit. Out-of-class activities may provide some of the best opportunities for spiritual growth which, when coupled with sound academic learnings, will help America and its citizenry to return to the level of values observed by Alexis De Toqueville on the occasion of his visit to America in the 1830s as reported at the beginning of this book, in its Preface: " . . . In America I found that (the spirit of religion and the spirit of freedom) were intimately united and that they reigned in common over the same country" (1), (p. iv).

Chapter VIII

Special Roles and Opportunities in Public Education for Reversing America's Moral and Spiritual Decline

A book of special interest to me is entitled *And Gladly Teach* (101), edited by Dr. James Smallwood, Professor of History at Oklahoma State University. It is a collection of reminiscences of Oklahoma teachers from "Frontier Dugout to Modern Module." Early in the book Smallwood observed:

> Individuals chose teaching careers for a variety of reasons. Rather than monetary considerations or status, most of those who wrote their reminiscences for this project stressed <u>service to their communities</u>, as a motive for teaching (101), (p. 15).

So many people, when asked who has been the most influential person in their lives will mention a former teacher or mentor— one of even greater influence than a parent in many cases. Emphasis is placed in the present chapter on the role of teachers and others especially close to students in values education both from the standpoints of <u>what they say</u> in their student contacts and <u>who they are</u> in relation to their students, day after day. In the pages that follow, the designation "teacher" will be used, on occasion, not only for those who are classroom teachers but also for others who work closely with students in out-of-class activities including athletic coaches, residence hall staff, and others who, although they may have limited contact with students, are highly student-oriented.

In his book, *The Art of Teaching* (102), Gilbert Highet lists several essentials of good teaching, one being "to like students." He continued:

> If you do not actually like boys and girls, or young men and women, give up teaching. A teacher must not only like the young because they are young. He must enjoy their company in groups. . . . Unless he likes groups of young people, he will not teach them well. It will be useless for him to wish that there were only two or three, or that they were all mature. They will always be young, and there will always be lots of them (102), (pp. 27, 28).

We live in a time of exciting new technological developments in education, including distance learning and the Internet. In the February, 1998 National Association of State Universities and Land-Grant College's *Newsline* (103) is an article by Graham Spanier, president of the Pennsylvania State University and chair of the NASULGC Commission on Information Technology, entitled "Information Technology's Impact on Higher Education." He noted that the single largest growth area for higher education in this country is in continuing and distance learning.

Along with the recognized, expanded learning opportunities and exposure to some of our brightest minds made possible by modern technology, some educators are concerned, however, about the reduction of opportunity for students to interact personally with their teachers. With the advent of television came "couch potatoes," and today there are those who are addicted to electronic learning devices, spending untold numbers of hours of learning without direct association with faculty and without the benefits generated through personal interaction. President

Spanier took note of this problem and suggested in the NASUL-GC *Newsline* statement (103):

> Instruction is becoming far more interactive. Email and other networking modes increase interaction between students and teachers and among students, changing the traditional one-way flow of communication from the professor.

In his September 4, 1998 *Newsletter* (104), NASULGC President C. Peter McGrath added the following:

> But information technologies and advanced communications are having and will have a major impact on how we teach, how we learn, and how we do research. They will bring change, but in no way can they replace human intelligence, individual questioning and skepticism, and the eternal quest for new information and knowledge. The transmission and application of these findings and insights is the unending mission of quality higher education (104).

Again, I would underscore the central thrust of this volume—the need for education to emphasize both mind and spirit with primary attention in the immediate future to the enhancement of the spiritual dimension which presently lags substantially behind the ever-increasing body of knowledge and its delivery systems.

This is not, however, a call to cut back on research and development—mainstays of the mission of Land-Grant universities and of universities generally. Far from it! It would be irresponsible to do such in view of the continuing needs to serve better (both in America, and throughout the world) those who are hungry, or homeless, or ill, or at war, or without purpose in life—to mention some of the persisting areas of human need that are not met adequately by present "know how." Actually, we must, to an extent beyond present efforts, become better able to serve humankind! As mentioned repeatedly, public education must also shoulder a greater responsibility than is now the case, acknowledging always the traditional lead roles of homes and churches in values education, to help them regain those lead roles as soon as possible.

A half century ago the American Council on Education, in its publication entitled "The Student Personnel Point of View" (4) emphasized the need for attention to students' spiritual development as part of their total educational experience. Considerable attention was given previously in Chapter IV of this volume to "The Student Personnel Point of View." Also mention was made earlier to an article by William H. Willimon, which appeared in the ACE Summer/Fall, 1997 issue of *Educational Record* (5), entitled "Religious Faith and the Development of Character on Campus" (14). Among his comments are the following:

> . . . People who are busy being religious—singing, praying, engaging in acts of devotion, serving the needs of others, listening to sermons, repeating their mantras, observing Kosher practices—often experience themselves becoming better people. Becoming a better person is a gracious by-product of praising and serving God.

It is also the observation of the author of *The Best of Mind and Spirit* that, for most people, an active spiritual life can be enriching and ennobling.

In a lead story in the December 10, 1998 issue of *The Daily Oklahoman* (105) was an article by David Briggs of the Religion News Service entitled "Want to Live a Longer Life? Then Go to Church on Sunday, Researchers Say" (105). The article went on to report that:

> A major study of church attendance and mortality reveals people who attend church weekly live an average of seven years longer than people who never attend worship services. Sociologists Robert A. Hummer of the Population Research Center at

The University of Texas, Christopher G. Ellison also of The University of Texas, Richard G. Rogers of The University of Colorado at Boulder, and Charles B. Nam of Florida State University made the findings (105).

To set the stage for the remainder of this chapter, let me restate my position; first, I am committed to a "free marketplace" in public education so far as the religious faiths of students, faculty and staff are concerned; and second, I believe educators at all levels of learning need to manifest the best of their respective faiths in their contacts with students. I do not, as already mentioned, propose the establishment of pulpits in classrooms for any one faith. I believe, however, that how we as educators speak and behave in our everyday relations with students can have a tremendous impact, for good or for bad, in the shaping of their values.

Let us begin with <u>love</u>—recognized, understood, and appreciated in varying degrees by peoples of virtually all faiths. Manifested fully, it is our greatest hope for coming to understand each other. It minimizes our differences and maximizes the possibilities of living together peaceably. Chapter 13 of I Corinthians in the New Testament of the Bible is known as the "love chapter." It was presented in its entirety in Chapter V.

Also, generally accepted and understood by most religions of the world is the Golden Rule, mentioned in both the Old and the New Testaments of the Bible. In the September, 1997 issue of the *Perspective Letter*, published by Concern Ministries of McLean, Virginia, is the following statement by Chris Halverson, editor (106):

> <u>There is a command from the hand of God</u>, passed down from the beginning of time. <u>It binds all people to a common code. It is the sum of all law to mankind.</u>
>
> To the Brahman it says: "Do naught unto others which would cause you pain if done to you."

(Mahabharate 5:1517).

And to the Buddhist it speaks: "Hurt not others in ways that you yourself would find hurtful." (Udana-Varga 5:18).

It teaches the Confucianist: "Do not unto others what you would not have them do unto you." (Analects 15:23).

And, it instructs the Taoist to: "Regard your neighbor's gain as your own gain and your neighbor's loss as your own loss." (Tai Shang Kan Ying P'ien).

The Zoroastrainist hears it said: "That nature alone is good which refrains from doing unto another whatsoever is not good for itself." (Dadistain-i-dinik 94:5).

And the Muslim knows it as: "No one of you is a believer until he desires for his brother that which he desires for himself." (Sunnah).

It tells the Hebrew: "What is hateful to you, do not to your fellowman." (Talmud, Shabbat 31a).

And by Jesus it is revealed: "Do unto others as you would have them do unto you." (Matthew 7:12).

How wise of God to enact a global decree, needing no other consultant than you. The way to treat others, we all would agree, is to follow the Golden Rule.

In the writing of *The Best of Mind and Spirit*, I have stated repeatedly the need for "the free marketplace" in public education for all religious faiths. As a Christian, I am better acquainted, however, with literature rooted in the Christian faith than I am with the writings of those of other faiths. Also, programs and activities related to the Christian faith are better known to me than are those of other faiths. Accordingly, in the pages that follow I shall give increasing attention to the thoughts and practices of my faith which have meaning in coping with the current values crisis in our nation. However, in keeping with my commitment to the free marketplace for those of all faiths in public education, <u>I invite and encourage all other faiths to manifest the best of their thinking and practices in dealing with America's current decline in its moral and spiritual values, as well as to join with those of all other faiths, as together we share in one great common effort to heal our current values malaise</u>.

I would repeat at this point an observation I made earlier in this chapter that <u>some teachers (even more than those of our homes and churches), are most influential in shaping the values of students</u>! Let me share some thoughts about the concept of vocation in relation to teaching. Generally, we consider vocation in terms of our daily work. We offer our students opportunities for "vocational guidance," toward the end that they, in the years ahead, might be meaningfully employed, commensurate with such considerations as their abilities, their personal qualities, and the availability of employment opportunities.

Webster speaks of "vocation" as: (a) a calling to a particular state, business, or profession; (b) regular or appropriate employment; and (c) a calling to the service of God in a particular station or state of life.

On the occasion of the 1959 national convention of the National Association of Women Deans and Counselors in Cleveland, Ohio, I presented an address entitled "Our Vocation is Students" (107). In my presentation were some thoughts expressed by Dr. Carl Michalson, professor of Systematic Theology, Drew University, from his book entitled *Faith for Personal Crises* (108). Because of their relevance to the present volume, Michalson's comments together with certain related ideas I expressed in the NAWDC presentation are included as Appendix D.[n] At this point I share the following thoughts of Michalson about a spiritual concept of vocation as presented in his book *Faith For Personal Crises* (108).

Michalson took note of the importance of work to us all, and discussed at some length the pressures and anxieties, the self-torture and aimlessness that characterize so much of our vocational life—the "pathology of vocational life." He explained the New Testament use of the word "vocation" as a calling to salvation and states further that "a man's life of faith is not suspended during working hours"—that one's vocational life is actually the arena in which God's calling is worked out (108), (p. 105).

Reference was made earlier in Chapter VII to an article by Thomas H. Groome in the February 10, 1998 issue of *The Christian Science Monitor* (93). I quote him additionally:

> All spiritualities also are convinced that the person is essentially spiritual, that the human vocation is to live in "right relationship" with God—however named—and with oneself, others, and creation.

In the December 25, 1992 issue of the *Denver Post* there was a magnificent statement by William Raspberry, a commentator on national affairs for the *Washington Post* writers group, entitled "Rediscovering the Power of the Spirit" (109), as manifested in the larger community's educational efforts beyond formal schooling. In his comments, Mr. Raspberry quoted Robert L. Woodson, Sr., Founder and President of the National Center for Neighborhood Enterprise in Washington, D.C. I share, in part, the wisdom of Mr. Woodson:

> Only recently has it crystallized for me that the one thing virtually all these successful programs had in common was a leader with a strong sense of spirituality. . . . I'm not saying the spiritually based programs always work, only that the successful programs always have a spiritual base (109).

In concluding his remarks, Raspberry added:

> I don't know how the details might work themselves out, but I know it makes as much sense to empow-

er those who have the spiritual wherewithal to turn lives around as to empower those whose only qualification is credentials (109).

Nat Holman, legendary star of the original Celtics and considered by many to be the dean of American basketball coaches of his time, learned the game on the playgrounds of New York's lower East Side. In a statement in a book written for Edward R. Murrow and edited by Edward P. Morgan entitled *This I Believe* (60), Holman spoke eloquently on the topic, "You Cannot Fix a Real Faith" (110). I quote in part:

> I realize that the responsibilities of any teacher are great and that those of a coach who spends more time with his pupils than any other teacher are even greater. Not only do I spend more time, but I feel emotionally closer to them, seeing and sustaining my students when they lose as well as when they win.
>
> . . . As a coach I have always tried to emphasize that winning is not enough. The game must be played right. I have often said that I would rather see my teams lose a game in which they played well than win with a sloppy performance that reflected no credit, except that it was sufficient to win. So I've tried to develop a way of thinking that sees life, and the things I do, as a whole, with every act relating to another set. This puts things in true perspective (60), (pp. 73,74).

There are so many good people whose lives are devoted to helping others. Nat Holman of New York City is but one of the many serving others. Mother Teresa certainly is an example of another who has given her life in service to others. In her book entitled *Meditations From a Simple Path* (111), she observed:

We are all God's children, so it is important to share

115

His gifts. Do not worry about why problems exist in the world—just respond to people's needs (111), (p. 72).

Whether in the classrooms of our schools or in working with gangs and drug addicts on the streets, or in serving the needy at home and abroad, the elements of helping those who hurt are much the same. <u>Love and spiritual faith are essential</u> wherever and in whatever form need exists. Religion can play a larger role than is currently understood and accepted by many people, including <u>millions of students in our public schools, pre-school through doctoral study.</u>

In Chapter VII (as well as elsewhere in *The Best of Mind and Spirit*) there is mention of <u>"the free marketplace" for those of all faiths</u> in public education institutions. Each one of us is free to worship and to manifest his or her own faith without dictation by others. Among other things, each religious group is free to share its literature with others. On some campuses, this is facilitated through the Office of Student Activities. Usually information stations are set up in the Student Union hallways or adjacent to sidewalks on campus. In my experience, many faith groups—Muslims, Buddhists, followers of Judaism, and Christians of various denominations—have used these opportunities.

Some faith groups provide special religious centers close to campus primarily to serve students of their own respective faiths. Traditionally, these have served students of the various Protestant denominations, Catholic students, and those of the Jewish faith. With the influx of great numbers of students of diverse faiths in recent decades, other religious centers are being added, such as Islamic centers for prayer, study, and worship. In situations where numbers in a particular group are too few to support their own facility, meetings often are held in reserved space on or off campus.

Some special off-campus ministries for international students were discussed in Chapter V. Those of many different faiths are attracted to the programs built on love, friendship, and a desire to be of help, whatever the special needs may be.

Although faculty and staff personnel may not promote any one faith in public education institutions, they (like their students) share in the "free marketplace" so far as religious expression is concerned. As an example, a "Fellowship of Christian Faculty and Staff" has existed for many years on the campus where I serve. Among its activities, the organization purchases space in the student newspaper on special occasions, such as the beginning of a new school year, Thanksgiving, Christmas, and Easter for publication of a spiritual message, together with a listing of faculty and staff members who share in underwriting the costs of the effort.

It should be noted that other faith groups also exercise their right to orient students to their respective faiths using the student newspaper and other means to publicize information.

Of special assistance to Christian faculty and staff in manifesting their faith in the public education setting is Christian Leadership Ministries (CLM), the higher education faculty ministry arm of Campus Crusade for Christ. The CLM publishes a quarterly magazine entitled *The Real Issue* (to which references have already been made). It provides for a sharing of thoughts of what may be done by Christian faculty and staff within the framework established by the First Amendment of the U.S. Constitution.

The director of Christian Leadership Ministries is Dr. Walter Bradley, formerly a professor of mechanical engineering for 30 years at Texas A&M University. Also serving fulltime as a national faculty representative for Christian Leadership Ministries is Dr. Rae Mellichamp, Emeritus Professor of Management, University of Alabama.

In the September/October, 1997 issue of *The Real Issue* (112) is an article by Mellichamp, entitled "How to Restore Christian Thought to the University." He noted that the answer is the Christian Faculty/Staff Fellowship. He stated additionally:

> I like to think of the fellowship in terms of a think tank, or research and development activity.

And, he continued:

> Broadly speaking, a faculty fellowship should accomplish two purposes. First, it is to be the means by which professors and staff determine how to affect students, colleagues, and the institution for Christ, and through which they cooperatively work to accomplish this end.
>
> Secondly, the fellowship should minister to the faculty and staff who constitute its membership. In this connection, the fellowship should promote and foster deep relationships between its members. It should impart vision to its members and equip them for the work of ministry. It should help members to pursue excellence in their work within the institution and within the larger community. And it should support and uplift members when they experience difficult times (112).

In the January 2, 1997 issue of CLM's *The Real Issue* (113) is an article entitled "Toward Integrating Your Life and Your Work," written by Dr. Edward L. Harris, Associate Dean of Administrative Affairs, College of Education, Oklahoma State University. He began by asking two questions: "Does your work matter to God? Is your vocation an integral part of who you are as a Christian?" He spoke of Christians "dividing their lives between Christian work and secular work"—of living in two worlds, "which not only takes a lot of psychological energy, but also jeopardizes their integrity." He added, "To live in two worlds sends mixed messages."

As an alternative to segmentation, Harris proposed the concept of integration of faith and work based on three principles: unconditional love, listening, and continual learning.

With regard to love, Harris stated:

> My job is to demonstrate love, cultivate a spiritually

attractive life, and clearly communicate the gospel message. I believe that God's job is to convict and convert. Do you love God with all your heart, soul and mind? Do you love your colleagues and students as you love yourself? Love is foundational for an integrated and effective Christian witness.

With regard to listening, he observed:

It's easy to have superficial relationships, and consequently, superficial conversation. I've noticed that many professors' conversations are more monologues than dialogues; one person attempting to get his or her point across. One of the great needs in effective communication is to learn how to listen. Listening allows us to practice unconditional love, for when we genuinely listen to people we communicate that they are important to us.

Finally, with regard to learning, Harris wrote:

To make an impact on our cultural context, we must be students of both God's word and the world in which we live. . . . Love, listening, and learning grow through conversations and shared experiences over time. They build a storehouse of memories which reinforces the relationship and serves as a context for sharing the gospel. Relationships grow when we ask God to cause them to prosper.

It is also important to understand the social environment in which we work and the worldview of our associates. In the context of love, listening, and learning we can better integrate our faith and our work. The professor's life should be one of prayer; prayer that we walk with wisdom and speak with grace, and for opportunities to spend creative time with our associates and integrate God's truth in our thoughts and activities.

As the result of a lifetime of association with people of faith as well as with some who have not chosen to participate in religious activities, I recognize some differences in the two groups, especially in their relationships with others. Earlier I presented an observation by William H. Willimon (14) as follows:

> . . . People who are busy being religious—singing, praying, engaging in acts of devotion, serving the needs of others, listening to sermons, repeating their mantras, observing Kosher practices—often experience themselves becoming better people. Becoming a better person is a gracious by-product of praising and serving God (14).

Additionally, as I served and observed my colleagues in UNESCO over a period of 17 months in 1977 and in 1978, I noted differences in the attitudes and contributions of those who brought spiritually-oriented positions to the conference table and those who did not. I noted also that there was a high degree of unanimity among the many different faiths of the 157 member nations at the time when issues aimed at improving the lot of humankind in the world were presented and discussed. I was impressed with how much we had in common and how, in so many ways, we are one family when considering the needs and the sufferings of people all over the world.

While serving in Paris, one of my colleagues on UNESCO's Executive Board was assassinated. A memorial service was held for him in UNESCO's main assembly hall with my counterpart from Japan, a Buddhist, Mr. Keitaro Hironaga, presenting a tribute. Many of the world's religions were represented on the Board (as well as those of no particular faith), but there was experienced a sense of reverence and oneness in the group on the occasion. I was impressed with the eulogy presented by my Buddhist colleague and friend who stated, "We look forward to seeing you, dear Brother, in heaven."

Up to this point, we have been concerned largely with our nation's values decline, as well as with some suggestions of what might be done in dealing with the problem in the present. We need also, however, to be thinking about what can and should be done in the years ahead, for the task which faces us is a monumental one—that of re-establishing in America a solid commitment to high moral and spiritual values together with restoring a way of life that reflects those values in all we think, say, and do. To be sure, there are some encouraging indicators of both awareness of the values crisis and "getting with it" in accomplishing some things to reverse our nation's present values decline. It is noteworthy that the need for emphasis on values education has been acknowledged in varying degrees by growing numbers of educational leaders in various academic fields of study, as well as by others in the world of work (business, engineering, law, and medicine, as examples).

In follow-up of the earlier discussion of the high and very special role of teachers (as well as of others of the faculties and staffs of education institutions) let us now give thought to some considerations which should receive special attention in teacher education programs.

As a first area for consideration by those contemplating a career in teaching (both in regular classrooms, and in related out-of-class activities in which students and staff have especially close working relationships), I propose that careful attention and orientation be given to the facts of America's current values crisis—morally and spiritually—essentially the problems and the implications of what is happening now, as presented in Chapter II of this volume. Also "the stage needs to be set" for a far greater involvement of public education in values education of young people today in view of the decline in the influence of homes and churches. Our public schools are so important and influential in the life of our nation; and they are best able to reach the masses of today's young people and to join with homes and churches in providing values education. As previously emphasized, efforts must be made as quickly as possible to restore the essential lead roles of homes and churches in values education. At this time, however, and probably from this time forward, public education must share to a greater extent than has been true in the past in our nation's overall efforts in moral and religious values education.

Private and parochial educational institutions are free, of course, to provide faith-based education. There is considerable misunderstanding, however, among some in public education about the role of religion in public education. As mentioned previously, the primary causes for confusion among those in public education stem largely from a lack of understanding of what the First Amendment of the USA Constitution says about religion in public life and how the Supreme Court has interpreted the First Amendment which states that: "Congress shall make no law respecting an establishment of religion, or prohibiting the free exercise thereof."

Benita Johnson, a good friend and neighbor, writing in the July 12, 1998 Stillwater *NewsPress* (114), observed:[h]

> Fact or Myth: The first amendment to the United States Constitution, through the Bill of Rights, prohibits prayer in the schools and, therefore, needs amending. Furthermore, the Supreme Court in 1962 outlawed prayer in school. And, finally, the Bible is banned from the shelves of public libraries and schools.

> These are all myths. The first amendment says "Congress shall make no law respecting an establishment of religion, or (it goes on to say) prohibiting the free exercise thereof . . ." Alex Adan in "Sorting Religion in Public," on May 7, 1995, in the *Tulsa World* said it best: "One of the most harmful and persistent myths is that the court, in 1962, outlawed prayer in school. Some people carry the misconception even further. You can still hear people

say the court 'took God out of the classroom.'" He goes on to say, "What the court did in 1962 was to prohibit the government (in this case the New York school board) from requiring recitation of a state-prescribed prayer in school . . . There was never a court decision that prohibited students from praying on their own initiative and in ways that did not impose on the rights of others."

The distinctions between state-endorsed or state-sanctioned religion and individual religion, without coercion, are made reasonably clear in, "Religion in the public schools: A Joint Statement of Current Law."

Published and endorsed by 35 religious organizations of all faiths and several other national organizations, it states that, "The Constitution permits much private religious activity in and about the public schools. Students have a right to pray individually or in groups or to discuss their religious views so long as they are not disruptive." And, "because the Establishment Clause does not apply to purely private speech, students enjoy the right to read their Bibles or other scripture, say grace before meals, pray before tests and discuss religion with other willing student listeners." However, it also says, "school officials may not mandate or organize prayer at graduation, nor may they organize a religious baccalaureate ceremony," and, "students may be taught about religion, but public schools may not teach religion." Finally, the Bible is on the shelves of public libraries and schools.

In the February-March, 1998 issue of the *American Bible Society Record* (115) was an article by Larry Jerden entitled "Bringing the Good News to America's School Children."[r] He wrote:

The Bible was once at the center of American education. That is no longer true. In recent times, controversy has restricted the scope of Scripture in public education.

Yet, in places as diverse as New Jersey, Michigan and Virginia, thousands of children in both public and private schools are learning that, as the Psalmist says, "The fear of the Lord is the beginning of wisdom." In fact, many youngsters take to the Scriptures as they would to the hottest new video game.

Just ask Diane Wagner. She works in northwest Virginia, teaching the Bible to public school children whose parents voluntarily sign them up for her monthly, 45-minute class—allowed by a legal "released-time" program. Wagner remembers the seventh grader who memorized 50 verses before Christmas break. And there was the third grader who last spring memorized more than 100 verses and was learning the entire book of Ephesians. "Some of our children really get into it," she says.

Release-time programs like hers (they meet off-campus during school hours) have twice been held constitutional by the U.S. Supreme Court and are legal in all 50 states. That legality permits thousands of public school students to memorize Bible verses and hear the Good News.

"When our students memorize John 3:16, we give them a Gospel of John," explains the Rev. Morgan Kinney, Chief Executive Officer of CBM Ministries, which conducts Bible study programs in various regions of the U.S. Kinney estimates that CBM workers have given out more than 44,000 ABS Scriptures in the 60 years of CBM work in Virginia.

What especially excites him is the positive response of parents who must sign a permission slip in order for their children to take part. "Even when the parents themselves don't go to church," he says, "they want their children to know the Bible."

CBM's rosters list more than 5,500 students enrolled in its Bible classes this year. The classes are held outside of public school buildings, but Kinney says that's not a problem. "We back our mobile classrooms up to the school property and bring the children to them."

There's no lack of interest on the part of most of the children. According to CBM's records, 92 percent of the public school students in one county participated. "In one school at times every child has attended," he adds.

Games, fun and prizes are part of CBM's curriculum, but serious focus is always given to Bible study. Kinney feels strongly about the classes because "we are raising the first biblically illiterate generation in American history. A high percentage of the children we serve have had no satisfactory understanding of the Bible. Many don't go to church, so the only exposure they receive to God's Word is what we give them."

"The Word is having a tremendous impact on these kids," says Wendell Lamb, a CBM instructor. "Three times this year we had adults that we ministered to as children bring their families to our church. They had strayed since childhood, but now have come back. I meet adults all the time who ask, 'Do you still do those Bible classes, Mr. Lamb?' I say, 'We do,' and they say, 'Well, I still remember John 3:16,' or 'Those classes sure meant a lot to me.'"

CBM's ministry also offers "Mailbox Club" Bible lessons, primary school versions of a Bible correspondence course, where top prize for memorizing Scripture is discounted tuition to a CBM Bible Camp.

Kinney notes that the camps "not only use the Gospels, but when the older kids get into deeper study, we have used ABS Bibles as well. We sure appreciate the subsidy ABS has given us."

In Caldwell, NJ, St. Aloysius Roman Catholic Church holds religious education classes for children on weekdays after school. The classes, called Confraternity of Christian Doctrine (CCD), teach the Bible along with doctrines of the Catholic Church.

"We have six classes of sixth grade students, 70 in all," reports Sister Alice Uhl, director of religious education. "Thanks to the ABS Grants Program, each student gets a copy of a CEV New Testament entitled Extreme Faith."

CCD teacher Ginger Loughney used ABS Bibles with her sixth grade students last year. This year, seventh grade teacher Elaine Chomko has them. "All my kids talk about," Chomko says, "is how much they like the ABS Bibles they got in Ginger's class."

The students' families also get touched by the Scriptures.

"The day I got the Bible," recalls John Shaw, 12, "I took it home and started to read it in our family room. My mom and dad walked in and so I started reading it out loud. We all thought it was kind of neat. Now we read it together."

God's Word is also reaching young hearts in Michigan. Some 1,700 students are enrolled in after-school Bible Clubs sponsored by Christian Service Clubs (CSC).

"Because we meet after school and rent the rooms from the school, there is no subsidy of religion by the state," explains CSC director Jan Lanser. Started 37 years ago, the Christian Service Clubs use ABS Gospels of Luke in their programs. And like their counterparts at CBM Ministries, the CSC staff are amazed at most children's lack of basic biblical knowledge.

To deal with that, the clubs have to be creative. Last year, for example, a club in West Michigan had members study the Gospel of Luke by pretending they were radio station WWJD (What Would Jesus Do).

Regardless of method or location, Bible study for school children is effective. Cadillac, Michigan Bible teachers Beth Stagg and Shirley Russ remember a girl, Kristyn, who began attending their club in October. The next month, she brought her brother. In December, he brought a friend. In January, his friend brought his sister. And in February, that sister brought a friend.

Christian educators find children are eager to hear and respond to the gospel. And the American Bible Society is there to help supply them with Scriptures.

The July 10, 1998 issue of *The Chronicle of Higher Education* included an article by Allison Schneider entitled, "Jane Tompkins's Message to Academe: Nurture the Individual, Not Just the Intellect" (116). The author noted that Ms. Tompkins wants colleges to focus on the self as well as the subject matter—to nurture the imagination, not just the intellect. And she added that Academe needs to do more than make a student marketable. It needs to educate "the whole human being"—mind, body, and spirit.

What are some other considerations and suggestions for those who wish to teach, whether directly in classrooms or in residence halls, through mentoring, counseling, or coaching, or through other teaching relationships that faculty and staff have with students? As emphasized earlier in this chapter, those who choose to teach must love students, regardless of the diversity of their personalities, ability levels, socioeconomic status, physical attractiveness, or behavior.

To digress for a moment, let me share from my teaching experiences subsequent to leaving the presidency of Oklahoma State University. Earlier in my career I taught younger students and became acquainted with their needs. Most of my more recent students, however, were studying at the doctoral level and were full-time educators themselves. A majority of them were married and had young families. I came to know and appreciate these highly committed, older, non-traditional students very much. Actually they were colleagues, in so many ways and they shared much from their own experiences and insights, all of which enriched the classes.

They were people with problems themselves—some similar to those of younger students and some unique to their own age group. After several years of serving these very special students, I prepared a paper specifically for them.[5] Even though the graduate level students were older and more sophisticated in many ways as compared with their undergraduate counterparts, I came to realize that they, too, needed affection.

It is essential that as a first consideration of those contemplating a teaching career there be discussion with teacher-education candidates of the necessity of loving all students, including some who may not be very lovable. Although most teachers rate high in manifesting love for their students, some do not, and may actually inflict damage to the personalities and the lives of the unloved. Those who do not have a genuine affection for students probably should not become teachers. (Actually, a service could be performed for all by helping those who do not give promise of being student-oriented to find a career more appropriate to their attitudes, abilities, and personal qualities.)

As a second consideration for those planning careers as teachers, attention should be given to America's current values decline together with discussion of the implications of such for the future—all against a backdrop, however, of America's continuing greatness and its basic goodness.

Most young people today, in their exuberance of life and in their enjoyment of the many good things associated with life in our richly blessed country, are really not aware of the seriousness of America's values decline. There is a need for educators (especially teacher-education mentors) to orient students to the realities of the current decline in America's values. Also, those who plan to teach need to be nurtured by their own teacher-educators in some special ways in view of their leadership responsibilities in years to come.

Third, those who plan to teach should be oriented to the high role of religion in values education in public education institutions. As has been mentioned throughout this volume, there is need for emphases on "the best of both mind and spirit," thereby acknowledging these two great influences in shaping the lives of individuals and nations—education and religion.

Earlier in this chapter, there was discussion of some facts and some myths in relation to the role of religion in public education about which there is much misunderstanding (114). The facts are that the First Amendment of our Constitution and certain Supreme Court decisions are more favorable to religion in public education than is commonly understood.

As a fourth suggestion, teachers generally (and especially those in teacher education programs) need to provide for teachers-to-be full and accurate information of what teachers may or may not do in emphasizing the importance of the spiritual dimension in one's total development. They need, also, to underscore the necessity of providing a "free marketplace" at all levels of public education, thereby assuring students, whatever their faiths may be, that they are free to live and to manifest their respective faiths fully in America as long as they do not violate the laws of their host nation.

I believe so strongly that matters of faith are essential in the shaping of what we think and say and do. Accordingly, I propose as a fifth recommendation, (as a companion to the establishment of "a free marketplace for all faiths" in public education), that administrators, teachers, and mentors of teachers-to-be encourage them to be active in the church of their choice. Because of the substantial influence teachers have in working with students, it is essential that teachers-in-training recognize this fact early and commit themselves to the highest and the best of which they themselves are capable. Teachers hold more than jobs! As mentioned earlier, theirs is a vocation in the highest spiritual terms.

As a sixth recommendation, teachers-to-be must recognize the fact that the needs of students differ. They must deal with each individual student accordingly, even in the face of such realities as large classes and less-than-adequate teaching conditions.

As I reflect on my own education, pre-school through doctoral study, I am reminded of how blessed I was with outstanding teachers—those who knew well their respective areas of knowledge, and who also made it a point to come to know each student individually. In relation to my pre-college days, I think of Miss Martin at the primary school level; Miss Landt and Miss Owens in middle school; and Coach Owen, Miss Silver (biology teacher), and Mr. Caldwell (physics teacher), in high school.

Although I did not know it at the time of my return to graduate study from WWII service in 1946, it was the beginning of my association with exceptional teachers, mentors, and colleagues who meant so much to me in preparing for my life's work, all great professionals in higher education and all people of religious faith.

Dr. C. Gilbert Wrenn was the major adviser for my Master of Arts degree in 1946 and my Doctor of Philosophy degree in 1948, both in counseling psychology. The adviser in my minor field of study, higher education, was Dr. Ruth Eckert. Both Dr. Wrenn and Dr. Eckert were highly competent and inspiring, as was Dr. Paul Meehl, from whom I took courses in abnormal and clinical psychology. All three, along with others, served on my doctoral committee.

Upon receiving my doctorate in 1948, I accepted the position of Dean of Students at Drake University where I served for seven years. It was at Drake University, under the tutelage of President Henry Harmon, that I experienced postdoctoral study in the area of practical aspects of administration not covered in my formal class work. I have always been grateful to President Harmon, a very helpful friend and mentor. He contributed so much to my preparation for subsequent service as Dean of Student Affairs and Dean of the Basic Division at Texas A&M University and as Dean of the College of Arts and Sciences, Vice President for Academic Affairs, and President of Oklahoma State University.

In the late 1950s and subsequently, I had the opportunity to serve on several American Council on Education Commissions and to work closely with Dr. Arthur Adams, President of the American Council on Education. How very helpful, and what an outstanding mentor and friend he was!

After becoming President of Oklahoma State University in 1966, I was privileged to become especially well-acquainted with two incumbent fellow presidents of universities with membership in the National Association of State Universities and Land-Grant Colleges—President Clement French of Washington State University and President Howard Bowen of the University of Iowa, both of whom were very helpful to me. How grateful I will always be to these two superb mentors—together with the others mentioned above, as well as others not listed.

One of my favorite books through the years has been *Through a Dean's Open Door* (117) by Dean Herbert E. Hawkes, long-time

Dean of Men at Columbia University. What is stated in Dean Hawkes' book helped to shape my philosophy and style of relating to students, faculty, and staff in my more than half a century of service in higher education as a teacher, counselor, and administrator. Regrettably, Dean Hawkes passed away shortly before his book was finished. Fortunately, however, Mrs. Hawkes, who shared her husband's "open door" philosophy, was able to finish the book. Following is the Introduction to *Through a Dean's Open Door*, by Irwin Edman, a long-time friend and associate of Dean Hawkes:

> The "open door" is a phrase that characterized the point of view and the educational policy of the late Dean Hawkes as well as anything could. It was a phrase often used by his colleagues, his students, and himself. His office door was always open when he was in his office; through *his* office one passed to that of his secretary. The open door described his mind and his method. Students and colleagues came always to a receptive, flexible, and hospitable spirit.

> This book describes some of the aspects of college education to which were freely admitted those who crossed the threshold of a mind for forty years open to growth and change in education (117), (p. v).

In April, 1963, I published an article entitled "Quality Teaching in Higher Education" (an abstract of an address presented at an earlier meeting of Oklahoma College and University Deans) which appeared in the *Oklahoma Teacher* (118), the professional journal of the Oklahoma Education Association. Among other things, I spoke of the need for high goals in higher education. Additionally, I urged that we need to take a hard look at the methods by which education takes place. I quoted J. Edward Dirks, editor of the journal, *The Christian Scholar* (119) as follows:

> . . . We may in fact need to be reminded that the way wherein we walk is itself part of the destination

toward which we move (119).

Following are some additional thoughts from Dr. Dirks' article entitled "Higher Education and Christian Conscience:"

> . . . In the relations of persons to subject-matters and to one another, the discipline of good behavior is often more telling than the idealism of high purposes. The open, good-humored, constantly self-examining and probing inquirer will bear the marks of a human sensitivity which will be educative in itself. The fearful, rigid, status-seeking, and embittered teacher, despite a high degree of learning, will erect barriers between himself and the creative process of education for human beings and a responsible human culture (119).

I conclude Chapter VIII (with its considerable emphasis on the high roles of both teachers and teachers-to-be in assuming leadership in reversing America's current decline in its moral and spiritual values) with a seventh proposal. I recommend that there be developed a carefully designed seminar or series of meetings to explore the essential role of values in all aspects of life to be required of all teacher education students. Such thoughts as I have presented earlier in *The Best of Mind and Spirit*, together with the thoughts of colleagues who are concerned about the decline in America's values and who understand what public education institutions may and can do within the law should be shared. Also, efforts need to be made by mentors in the overall preparations of teachers to underscore the need for their students to be active and to lead in efforts to reverse the present decline in our nation's moral and spiritual values as part of the larger, on-going efforts of many in the millennium into which we have recently entered.

Any course that might be developed should be rigorous in its demands, as well as relevant in dealing with the subject. In no way should it be a "patsy" course. A lead teacher who understands the seriousness of our nation's present values crisis, and who is committed to provide creative leadership in coping with the situation should be selected, together with several committed and qualified colleagues to assist in both designing and implementing the program.

Student discussion should be encouraged as part of the course, with those of different faiths sharing their perspectives relative to the enhancement of moral and religious values. Attendance and examinations would be required.

In proposing the establishment of a program as just discussed, I would underscore once again that homes and churches must continue to be acknowledged, encouraged, and supported as the lead agencies in values education. The current lessening in the influence of homes and churches cries out, however, for public education institutions (pre-school through doctoral study) to do more in values education, especially in view of their ability to reach the masses of young people today and the opportunity they have to present concurrent emphases on both academic and spiritual matters—the best of both mind and spirit.

Chapter IX

Some Additional Proposals for Dealing with America's Moral and Spiritual Decline

Primarily in Chapter II and to a lesser extent throughout this volume, consideration is given to the various elements in America's current moral and spiritual values decline. The lessening of the influence of homes and churches in values education has been noted repeatedly. Also, considerable emphasis has been placed on the need for public education (as well as such other agencies as the various media, the courts of our land, and the entertainment industry) to become more aware of the seriousness of what is happening to our values in America, as well as the need for all to join with homes and churches in efforts to reverse the present values decline.

As we begin this final chapter of *The Best of Mind and Spirit* let us consider some additional thoughts about homes and churches regaining their previous lead roles in values education. In the October, 1995 issue of Hillsdale College's publication *IMPRIMIS* (120)[d] is an article by Patrick F. Fagan, Fitzgerald Fellow for Family and Cultural Studies at the Heritage Foundation in Washington, D.C., entitled "The Real Root Cause of Violent Crime: The Breakdown of the Family." He affirms four simple principles: First, marriage is vital; second, parents must love and nurture their children in spiritual as well as physical ways; third, children must be taught how to relate to and empathize with others; and, finally, the backbone of strong neighborhoods and communities is friendship and cooperation among families.

In the June, 1997 issue of *IMPRIMIS* (121)[d] is an article by Dr. Wade F. Horn, a clinical psychologist and director of the National Fatherhood Initiative, Washington, D.C., entitled "Why There is No Substitute for Parents." He noted that whereas in 1969 the total number of children living in fatherless homes was fewer than eight million, there were nearly 24 million in 1997!

With regard to the role of fathers, Horn emphasized (121):

> First, our culture needs to replace the idea of the superfluous father with a more compelling understanding of the critical role fathers play in the lives of their children, not just as "paychecks," but as disciplinarians, teachers, and moral guides.

> Second, we need to convey the importance and sanctity of marriage. While more boys and girls expect that they will eventually get married and have children, they no longer believe that there needs to be a chronology to these two events. They should be taught that marriage comes first and that it is not a trial arrangement that can be abandoned whenever conflicts arise. Here's where religious and moral instruction can make a huge difference.

> Third, we must make restoring the rights and responsibilities of parents a national priority. Over the past century, child rearing has increasingly come to be viewed as a public rather than a private matter. As early as 1901, the Supreme Court of Indiana upheld a compulsory education law by arrogantly declaring, "The natural rights of a parent to the custody and control of his children are subordinate to the power of the state."

The tide is turning, however. Even many die-hard critics of the traditional family have finally been forced to admit that their ivory tower theories are wrong; in the real world, children need to be raised by two parents.

Horn called on communities to do more, also—and there are some encouraging things happening in our communities at this time. In the April, 1999 issue of the *NRTA Bulletin*, (a publication of the National Retired Teachers Association) is an article by Neal Gregory, a Washington, D.C. based freelance writer, who spoke about "Keeping America's Promise—Powell-Led Army Mobilizing to Help At-Risk Youth."[t] Gregory observed (122):

> Retired Gen. Colin L. Powell's main job today is serving as chairman of America's Promise—The Alliance for Youth, a nonprofit group he helped launch two years ago this month at a highly publicized "summit" in Philadelphia headed by President Clinton and former presidents Bush, Carter and Ford.[u]
>
> After shaking off some start-up problems, the organization now seems to be on a roll, and Powell is clearly the force driving it. At stake, as he sees it, are the lives of some 15 million youth who are "vulnerable to drug abuse, gangs, violence, premarital sex and other social pathologies."
>
> "What we have to do with our young people is give them a sense of purpose and vision," he says, "a belief in themselves, a belief in the country." Although he has voiced words like these many times, he speaks with obvious feeling.
>
> America's Promise, he explains, does not operate any youth services; rather, it serves as a catalyst— "a Johnny Appleseed"—to add new muscle to such

long-established organizations as Big Brothers and Big Sisters of America, Save the Children, and Junior Achievement.

America's Promise has five highly specific goals: to promote more mentoring of young people, to give them safe places and structured activities after school, to foster their good health, to give them marketable skills and, as Powell puts it, "to let [young people] know that we have expectations for them" and that they must give something back to their communities. "We didn't come this far to have the next generation blow it," he says bluntly (122).

I would note, at this point, that increasing numbers of our churches (the ones to which growing numbers of young people are attracted today) are underscoring the <u>need for a strong spiritual base in dealing with today's problems</u>. In addition to learning of God's love, grace, and forgiveness, they also learn of what's right and what's wrong, and about certain absolutes such as the Ten Commandments. They learn that God is a God of judgment as well as a God of love and forgiveness, and that turning away from His precepts will lead to disaster for humankind. They learn that "the fear of the Lord is the beginning of knowledge" (Proverbs 1:7, NIV). (The definition of "fear" as used above is "reverential awe of God.") They learn of spiritually-based answers as to how to deal with the problems of the times in which they live—times of decline in society's values not unlike those of which the prophet Jeremiah spoke in the Old Testament of the Bible:

Hath a nation changed their gods, which are yet no gods? But my people have changed their glory for that which doth not profit.

Be astonished, O ye heavens, at this and be horribly afraid, be ye very desolate, saith the Lord.

For my people have committed two evils; they have forsaken me the fountain of living waters, and hewed them out cisterns, broken cisterns, that can hold no water (Jeremiah 2:11-13).

Unfortunately, there are some churches in our time that have "hewed out broken cisterns that can hold no water." We should be encouraged, however, in view of the commendable efforts of others of our churches, as they cope with today's decline in our nation's moral and spiritual values.

There is need for churches to do some things differently than in the past, however, in their efforts to reach people today. In some non-traditional situations, such as those where both parents work, there is need for a more relevant ministry, especially in the reaching of young people and in getting them involved in church, education, worship, social, and service activities. (I would note at this time that putting spiritual faith to work in helping those that are less fortunate has a special appeal for many young people.)

We need also to take note and to give credit to those churches that do have strong outreach programs that provide moral and spiritual nourishment for both givers and recipients. An example is the Oklahoma United Methodist "Circle of Care, Inc." (123), established in response to Jesus' statement that "whoever welcomes a little child like this in my home welcomes me."

The Circle of Care has in fact been serving young people for more than eight decades. Its current executive director is Mr. Tom Campbell. Following is a list of its present service agencies: Boys Ranch at Gore, OK; Children's Home at Talequah, OK; Community Services including counseling services, adoption services, crisis pregnancy counseling, and Child S.A.R.E. at Oklahoma City, OK; Frances Willard Home for Girls, Tulsa, OK; Holsinger Home, Enid, OK; and Woodward Counseling Center, Woodward, OK.

I would note additionally that many other denominations have similar programs of outreach.

Charles Trueheart, in a well-researched article in the August,

1996 issue of *The Atlantic Monthly* entitled "Welcome to the Next Church" (124) reported on his study of new, non-traditional churches which, in his words, are "drawing lots of people, including many Americans with patchy or blank histories of churchgoing" (124). It is a report that, hopefully, will be read by many.

Mr. Trueheart spent a year researching the wide-variety of "Next Churches" in action. He described in some detail one of the many visited, the Mariners Church at Newport Beach, California. Included in *The Atlantic Monthly*[v] report were the following observations:

> I approached Mariners Church, on a gentle hill above Newport Beach, California, through its parking lot. At the entrances to the asphalt expanse men and women in reflective orange jackets waved on a procession of hundreds of cars entering by twos the acres of parking places being vacated by the outflow from the earlier service. Mercifully, confusion did not reign (124).

> The new architecture of faith is inconspicuous. The seven-year-old sanctuary of Mariners is an understated horizontal brick pile with barely a peak in its auditorium roof, let alone anything suggesting a spire. Walking from my car, I realized that no door to the church building was visible—a mischievous design considering that Mariners, like other churches of this ilk, has figurative doors that are uncountable. And on the side away from the parking lot are real glass ones constantly admitting people—these days 3,500 at four services every weekend, and many hundreds more during the week. The Next Church rarely sleeps. (124).

> The doors of Mariners open onto a tree-lined semi-circular courtyard that was packed that Sunday morning with hundreds of people standing and talk-

ing together in the sunshine. A few, wearing name tags, approached and shook hands with everyone arriving; in the case of a stranger they gave a simple friendly greeting and no more. An orchestra played upbeat soft rock somewhere within wafting melody and song to the outside. The dress was California casual. Children scurried everywhere. A cappuccino cart with parasol stood to one side, dispensing the secular sacrament. And along the periphery of the courtyard one shaded table after another announced the church's various "ministries," support groups, and fellowship opportunities—each a point of entry into the Mariners community (124).

We heard from the forty-one-year-old senior pastor of Mariners, Kenton Beshore, who spoke discursively and often wittily on "Enclaves and Community." One riff caught my attention. It drew on the Scriptures: "I will build my church, and the gates of Hell will not stand against it." Beshore explained to his flock, "Hell wants to build walls all around this church, and every church in our community, so the world doesn't see. It doesn't see our love and fellowship . . . it doesn't see our unity." . . . Following Saint Paul's first letter to the Corinthians, they seek to be "all things to all men"—not forgetting the rest of the sentence, "that some might be saved." By taking on roles as various as those of the Welcome Wagon, the USO, the Rotary, the quilting bee, the book club, the coffee shop, and the mixer— and, of course, the traditional family and school— they have become much more than the traditional churches that many Americans grew up in and have long since lost. Belonging to Mariners or any other large church conveys membership in a community, with its benefits of friends and solace and purpose and the deep satisfaction of service to others (124).

Later in the article, the author, Charles Trueheart, shared the following statement: (124).

> When we were talking in his office one day, Beshore described the Next Church strategy as succinctly as I was to hear it: "We give them what they want," he said, "and we give them what they didn't know they wanted—a life change" (124).

To some, the emergence of "next churches" such as Mariners presents a threat. Although I have been active in a much more traditional Methodist Church for most of my life, I have become aware that large numbers of people are being attracted to and served by non-traditional churches such as Mariners. They are reaching many who are unchurched, including great numbers of young people who are for the first time learning about God, His Son Jesus, and the Holy Spirit at work in their lives, and in the world.

In our travels around the world, my wife Maxine and I have been privileged to worship at sea and on land with those of many different nationalities, colors of skin, and patterns of worship— all deeply committed, however, in their praise and adoration of God. Some of the most enthusiastic worshipers were those in Thailand and Korea. Places of worship ranged from a very modest frame church in Ethiopia, to the magnificent Cathedral in Christchurch, New Zealand, where we shared in Easter services.

While in Jerusalem (with the concurrence and assistance of my Jewish guide) I was privileged to pray at the Wailing Wall.

With the world headquarters of the United Nations Educational, Scientific, and Cultural Organization (UNESCO) headquartered in Paris, protestants of many nations join in worship at the American Church in Paris, described as follows in its church bulletin:

> This church is a unique example of Christian unity

in action. Being the first American church established on foreign soil, it is the oldest non-governmental American institution abroad. Many denominations and nationalities are represented in its membership.

A cherished memento of our worship experiences while in Paris is a copy of *The Hymnal* (125), "Published by Authority of The General Assembly of the Presbyterian Church of the United States of America" in 1933. Out of consideration and respect for those from other lands that worship at American Church, some hymns of other nations and of other Protestant traditions are included in *The Hymnal* (125).

A most welcome and delightful volume about present day activities in our churches is Boyce Bowdon's book entitled *The Child Friendly Church* (126), a 1999 publication in which the author discussed "150 Models of Ministry with Children in Churches Throughout America."

To return to an earlier discussion (in Chapter II), I would underscore the need for churches to assume greater responsibility for sex education and counseling to supplement the present less-than-adequate efforts of various agencies in serving this overwhelming need. Tragically, most young people are pretty much on their own so far as matters of sex education are concerned. Homes and churches, as emphasized often in this volume, must again take the lead; but, as also repeated throughout this book, they need to be joined by our schools, with emphasis on the wisdom of abstaining from pre-marital sex until marriage vows are taken and commitments made to each other by the marriage partners.

In so many ways, the wisest investment of our time and money would be to have homes, churches, and schools join in efforts to assure counsel for each and every student about responsible sex, marriage, and child-rearing. Some will say, "We cannot afford such!" Actually, we cannot afford not to do as proposed. We must deal forthrightly with the current "wide-open" sex behavior problem in America—in many ways, the most decadent element in our society's current values malaise.

Many good people recognize the need to take steps to rise above the present level of relatively uninhibited sexual behavior but do not manifest the courage to join with others who are also concerned. Our spiritual beliefs, commitments, and behaviors have much to offer young people in the achievement of healthy, satisfying, and lasting sexual experiences. However, we have not as yet come together in a shared, concerted effort of homes, churches, schools, and other concerned social agencies, in providing spiritually-oriented sex education and counseling for our nation's young people.

Moving on to a different subject, I believe that many students from middle schools through college years who have experienced sound home and church values education could be of help in assisting those of their fellow students who have been denied positive home and church influences in shaping their values. Tragically, so many of our young people have little or no basis for judging that which is right and that which is wrong. Recognizing such, I would propose that selected <u>peer groups of spiritually-oriented students</u> join with student-oriented and spiritually-oriented faculty and staff in making available to students within their acquaintance (who come voluntarily) <u>counsel relative to the role of the spiritual dimension in their education</u>, and subsequently, <u>in the establishment of their own homes and their employment</u>. It might all start with coke dates, one on one, and later move to larger fellowship group meetings, and to worship in a church of each individual's choice.

Earlier in this volume, in Chapter IV, reference was made to an article by Jon C. Dalton and Anne Marie Petrie, entitled "The Power of Peer Culture" (76), which appeared in the Summer/Fall 1997 issue of *Educational Record* (5), a former publication of the American Council on Education).

The following quotation is from the Dalton and Petrie article:

Any serious effort to promote the moral and civic

character of college students must, at some point, come to terms with the powerful shaping influence of the college peer culture. Like an invisible invader, the influences of peer culture permeate almost all aspects of students' lives and enhance or erode the best educational efforts of faculty and administrators. In recent research on college students, Alexander Astin concluded that the single most important source of influence on the individual student is the peer group.[w]

The most damaging effects of student peer culture in college involve excessive alcohol and drug use, sexual exploitation, incivility, conformity, and materialism. The negative and conforming influence of peer culture all too often depreciates the educational goals of moral and civic responsibility. Despite the sophisticated efforts of colleges and universities to guide and shape students' values and morals, students nevertheless seem to move relentlessly in the direction of the dominant orientation of the peer group, which can be negative. It also can be positive (76).

The concluding observation in the quote just mentioned, that "It also can be positive" (76), provides the direction in which peer groups can and must move in enhancing the level of moral and spiritual values of today's young people.

Reference was made in Chapter II to an article in the January 12, 1998 issue of *Christianity Today* (45) written by Frederica Mathewes-Green,[x] a former abortionist, in which she shared her thoughts relative to "Wanted: A New Pro-Life Strategy." She discussed the problem as one who has championed both sides of the abortion issue in her lifetime—first as a young woman and a college student desiring liberation and later as one who converted to the pro-life position after coming to realize (in her own words) "that the being in the uterus was more than a blob of tissue, that it could be a human life that wanted to go on living." No longer could she say that abortion was right, but neither was she ready "to jump on the anti-abortion bandwagon." What she did come up with was a new strategy based, first of all, on <u>listening</u>, followed by <u>persuasion</u> as explained in the following from the January 12 issue of *Christianity Today*:[h]

> The first step in adopting the <u>persuasion</u> model may sound surprising: Put the question of making abortion illegal on the back burner. I believe abortion should be illegal because it is violence against the smallest members of our human family. But one of the reasons we're stuck in a deadlock is because political posturing has overwhelmed the moral discussion.

The second point in the author's persuasion model was that abortion hurts women. She observed:

> It is important to press the point—in what sense does a woman want this? No one saves up, hoping one day to have an abortion. It costs hundreds of dollars, money anyone would surely prefer to spend elsewhere. The procedure itself is physically unpleasant, humiliating, and often painful. Do we really believe that women want this?

> Women don't <u>want</u> abortions. They are expensive, awkward, humiliating, painful, and potentially dangerous. And we have not yet considered the most compelling effect: abortion breaks a woman's heart. At some level, she knows it is her own child who is dying, a son or daughter who looks as much like her as any she will carry full term.

The third point made by the writer was that we can live without abortion. She stated that there are two problems to solve in order to advance that case. The first is preventing unplanned pregnancies in the first place, and the second is giving women support when they do become pregnant so they will not opt to abort.

She continued:

> When sex occurs between two people who have no lasting commitment to each other, a resulting pregnancy is likely to be "unwanted." Recovering an ethic of commitment-based sexuality will mean rediscovering the value of chastity before marriage. The True Love Waits movement is a good example of how this new sexual ethic can be held up and encouraged.

Frederica Mathewes-Green concluded her article with the following:

> When these three points are covered, listeners will often say, "I agree with you; I just don't think it should be illegal."
>
> Since there is no present opportunity to make abortion illegal anyway, when the topic does come up, let's avoid the temptation to let the conversation get hijacked into a polarizing discussion that offers no practical application. A more realistic goal for pro-life advocates is to bring about, through both active listening and gentle persuasion, a gradual dawning of the conviction that we can live without abortion. Eventually that may result in a cultural consensus to make it illegal once more.
>
> So our ultimate goal, in all of this reevaluation, remains the same: to end legal and social acquiescence to this atrocity. In America, there is an irreducible core of laws that we could not live without, without which we would have barbarism. These are the laws against violence—child abuse, rape and

murder, spouse-battering. These laws are sometimes the only thing that stand between the small
and weak and the strong and powerful. And abortion laws are that kind of law. Unborn children are
the smallest members in our human family, and they
deserve that protection.

Opponents of abortion laws tend to envision a perfect society where women are empowered and free,
arguing that a few legally permitted abortions (37
million?) is the price we must pay to get there. But
can a just society really be founded on the death of
children? How many deaths can we tolerate in pursuit of this utopian vision?

Earlier in this volume, in Chapter II, introductory comments
were made relative to the magnitude of the alcohol and drug
abuse problem among America's youth. Additionally, in Chapter
IV, there is discussion of some steps taken by the American
Council on Education and by the National Association of State
Universities and Land-Grant Colleges in relation to alcohol and
drug problems.

President C. Peter McGrath, in his June 1, 1998 letter to the
leadership of the NASULGC (127), spoke as follows:

I want to comment on a frustrating and treacherous
issue: alcohol abuse. All of you out there on our
campuses, and most especially our residential universities, are well aware of the appalling episodes
that have taken place this spring at some of our
most distinguished universities. There is nothing
new here: alcohol abuse and the vulgarity that
accompanies it, was prevalent during my years as an
undergraduate student in the 1950s. It is also clear
that this is not a narrow college problem but a
national social problem. But to say this does not
excuse us from reexamining all of our policies and

practices with regard to alcohol toleration. We should, I believe, consider such steps as insisting (even if it will never be close to 100 percent effective) that alcohol never be served at campus events when underage students are present.

The alcohol abuse problem should be a visible pre-occupation of presidents and academic leaders in the same way that we surely believe that speaking out against racial injustice and other forms of discrimination is an important part of our moral leadership responsibilities. I certainly do not have the answers nor the wisdom to prescribe the "best" solution, but I am pleased that at its next meeting the NASULGC Board of Directors will endorse a strong resolution on alcohol abuse proposed by our student affairs officers. We can no longer cop out by saying that this is a problem larger than our universities (of course it is) or by allowing alcohol interests, subtly and financially, to influence our policies through various endorsements that we implicitly and tacitly give, or by even buying into the argument that college drinking is a rite of passage. Surely, we all know that education, learning, and alcohol are hardly interrelated parts of our educational curriculum!

The NASULGC statement, to which reference was just made and which was passed by NASULGC's Board of Directors, reads as follows:

The student affairs professionals through NASULGC, the National Association of Student Personnel Administrators, and the American College Personnel Association, endorse and strongly support the efforts of fraternities and sororities to change their alcohol-dominated culture and to

149

develop alcohol-free living environments by fall 2000.

It concludes by stating that

> . . . senior student affairs officers and their staffs (should) become more directly involved as catalysts for positive culture change on their campuses and in their Greek communities by engaging students in partnership with faculty, staff, and community citizens through positive norming, strong values statements, and change strategies.

Sometimes conditions have to become worse before getting the attention of those responsible. A *U-WIRE* report out of Evanston, Illinois (128), indicated that:

> The National Panhellenic Conference passed a resolution October 17, 1998 endorsing substance-free fraternities and encouraging their 26 member sororities to participate in alcohol-free events with them.

At the same time, it was reported that several national fraternities had already decided to eliminate alcohol in their chapter houses, and that others will soon follow, according to Greek leaders.

Others from off the campuses are also taking strong stands against drinking on campuses. According to a *U-WIRE* release out of State College, Pennsylvania (129), Act 199, a state law went into effect February 18, 1998. It included restrictions on advertising alcoholic beverages in yearbooks, newspapers, program books, brochures, and similar publications published by or for educational institutions.

Additionally, according to an *Associated Press* report out of Atlanta (130), United States Health and Human Services Secretary Donna E. Shalala, in an address January 12, 1998, challenged university presidents, chancellors, and other delegates to the NCAA national convention to cut ties between college athletics and drinking. She emphasized the need to fight youth alcohol abuse and urged those in attendance to assume leadership. She observed:

> ...binge-drinking is sweeping campuses "with a vengeance," leading to assaults, date rape, car wrecks, permanent health problems and deaths.

> "Our messages about the dangers of alcohol are not getting through to older teens," she said.

> While not blaming the problem on college sports, she said the battle against alcohol abuse would be boosted by "breaking the connection between sports and drinking."

> She urged tough voluntary guidelines: no alcohol advertising at collegiate sporting events, no alcohol-related sponsors, no bringing alcohol to games, and no "turning a blind eye" to underage drinking at tailgate parties and elsewhere around sports events.

> She cited professional baseball's campaign against smokeless tobacco as helping result in a decline of new tobacco-chewers among young people. Certainly, her words and efforts should be applauded!

As previously indicated, the National Association of State Universities and Land-Grant Colleges is now engaged in a self-examination of drinking on member campuses. The Kellogg Commission on the Future of State and Land-Grant Universities as noted in Chapter IV, has been at work on a five-part study. Their first report, entitled *Returning to Our Roots—The Student Experience* (3), was published in 1997. It was recommended in that report that emphasis be placed on healthy learning environments. One statement in the first report is especially relevant to the current discussion of alcoholic problems, and is repeated at this time:

> If there is a more unhealthy factor on campus today than excessive consumption of alcohol, we cannot

identify it. Both research and anecdotal evidence indicate that alcohol is often involved in the difficulties and tragedies students encounter (3).

Although other factors and causes contributing to our nation's current values decline (together with how to deal with them) might be presented individually in this closing chapter, I have chosen to cluster a number of them in view of a common denominator—that being the subject of "freedom of expression," whether in the form of printed media, television, Internet/Web programming, or the entertainment industry.

We live in a highly permissive time where seemingly "anything goes." Since America's founding, freedom of expression has been cherished and has been protected by our courts—although in some cases there have been decisions of our courts that have been questioned by many citizens. Early in my life, I came to respect the wishes of the majority (as well as of the minority, which also should be heard) with decisions ultimately made on the merits of the positions taken. In most cases, majority thinking has prevailed, although in recent years it has been my observation that there has been a leaning in favor of individuals' rights. Whether concerning materials of a pornographic nature, the use of profanity, or offensive language in generally poor taste, the position of the majority of citizens has not always prevailed. Again, I strongly believe in the rights of individuals but I also believe that we are free to do only the responsible thing—that which is good, considerate of the rights and the feelings of others, in good taste, and within the law.

Let us now consider some problems associated with television programming. In the May 1998 issue of the *NRTA Bulletin* (131), the magazine of the National Retired Teachers Association, Susan L. Crowley wrote about "Minow's Long Campaign to Improve TV for Kids."(y) She observed:

> In 1961, President Kennedy's eager young Federal Communications Commission chairman seared himself into public memory by declaring television

a "vast wasteland."

Now, 37 years after Newton Minow stunned broadcasting executives with that blunt critique, the wasteland, he maintains, is bleaker than ever.

"The level of programs, particularly for children, has deteriorated," says Minow. "There is more violence, more sex, more unpleasantness than ever before."

The writer continued: (131).

Given the fact that many kids spend more time in front of a TV than in school, Minow says, the continuing prevalence of junk programming is a "major disappointment."

Nonetheless, Minow, even after nearly 40 years, isn't about to give up jawboning lawmakers and broadcasters to improve television for children.

"Television is so important, so valuable," he says, "that it's frustrating when the medium doesn't fulfill its potential to inform, instruct, uplift."

And Susan Crowley added: (131).

He is unmoved by arguments that regulating children's shows violates free-speech rights of the First Amendment.

Continuing, the writer reported: (131).

Even children's TV has had its high points, he adds, during for example, the golden age of the 1940s and 1950s, with programs like "Captain Kangaroo," "Lucky Pup," "Howdy Doody," and Minow's personal favorite, "Kukla, Fran and Ollie."

Ironically the only standards for children's TV were developed in 1952 by the industry itself, through the

National Association of Broadcasters (NAB), which also restricted commercial time on kid's shows.

The NAB code, along with heavy lobbying by child advocates, resulted briefly in better programs in the 1970s.

Then "in a moment of madness," Minow says, the courts in 1982 knocked out the code by ruling that it violated antitrust laws by curtailing commercial time on children's shows.

The deregulatory era of the early 1980s hastened the demise of quality programs, Minow says. With market forces in full play, entire shows were created around products like Hot Wheels, Mighty Morphin Power Rangers and Teenage Mutant Ninja Turtles.

Children nonetheless have been able to take refuge in vaunted programs like public broadcasting's "Sesame Street," "Mr. Rogers' Neighborhood" and "The Magic School Bus." Minow also cites the Nickelodeon cable channel as an example of a profit-making venture that turns out good kid programs. Even so, the number of raunchy, bloodthirsty and just plain mindless shows keeps spiraling upward on network and cable channels. But parents and grandparents have some recourse, says Minow.

Such as heeding rating of shows. Although the system launched last year that uses codes to caution viewers about sex, violence and profanity in programs is "unnecessarily complicated," Minow says, it's worth giving it a try. He also favors the development of other rating services, "so a parent can choose."

Then there are v-chips, designed to work with ratings and to block offensive programs, but their success depends on how good rating systems are and on parental know-how. "The kids know more about [technology] than the parents," Minow says, and could bypass the chips.

Predictably perhaps, the v-chip has triggered protests that by locking out selected programs, it violates First Amendment rights.

"It seems to me all it does is give a parent a remote control unit," Minow says. "People forget—the First Amendment is a restriction on the government, it is not a restriction on parents."

If Minow is battle weary, he doesn't show it. In fact, he was recently named to a presidential commission that will spell out public responsibilities of broadcasters in the coming age of digital TV.

He still sees television as a tool of enlightenment and doesn't go along with people who say they are so fed up, they don't even own a television set.

"If they say that, they're missing life," Minow says (131).

Television may be the most targeted medium in relation to impropriety. Many of the concerns expressed, however, apply also to the print media, radio presentations, some library holdings, certain Internet/Web programming and the entertainment industry generally. There is an encouraging number of people within the various media, however, who are at work to reduce the extent of offensive materials and activities to which people of all ages are exposed. They must, of course, as Newton Minow comments on efforts to improve TV programming for children, "keep the faith" and continue to work for higher and more acceptable standards of programming.

One such person in the film production industry is Jimmie

Baker, an alumnus of Oklahoma State University and a veteran of more than 50 years with ABC Television. He is now the retired head of Jamie Productions (132). In a 1998 visit with him, he shared with me that a few years ago a minister by the name of Larry Poland came to ABC-TV in Hollywood and asked him to help get a group of people together from the major film and television studios for the purpose of bringing more family and moral TV and film shows to the viewing public. This was done, with the result that "THE KEYMEN" organization was established to provide leadership in upgrading the moral level of films. It has become a moving force in Hollywood. Jimmie told me I would be amazed at the number of Christians who have "come out of the closet" at the major studios, not only in Hollywood, but in New York City, Chicago, and other cities. He reports that "THE KEYMEN" have grown "by leaps and bounds." He said, "We are all over the United States, and still growing."

Reflecting on the many and varied problems that have contributed to America's current values crisis as discussed in earlier chapters, there are models demonstrated in the efforts of the Newton Minows and the Jimmie Bakers that might well be followed by other concerned people and agencies in helping to reverse our nation's values decline. I have no doubt that if the energies and the talents of the many concerned good people of America were harnessed and joined together in a great common effort, the impact and influence of the negative forces would be reduced substantially.

I believe there are good people in all walks of life, people who, if knowledgeable about the facts and given proper leadership and support, will work for the best of both mind and spirit. I believe also that many of the factors mentioned as contributing to our nation's values decline are generated by agencies that are potentially among the best ones to help restore a higher level of values in America. We need to be mindful of and grateful for the positive things now being done by people in government, in the press, in business and industrial enterprises, in the courts, in education, in the entertainment world, in rural America, in our cities of all sizes, and most importantly, <u>in our families and churches</u>.

Throughout this volume, it has been acknowledged repeatedly that homes and churches <u>have been and must continue to be</u> the lead agencies in values education of our children and young people, and that all other agencies need to join <u>in support</u> of addressing that need. So many things may and can be done by other agencies—especially by our public schools—in support of homes and churches, as well as, in providing to some degree for the special needs of those young people who are not now privileged to be receiving values education from homes and churches.

In Chapter II, I commented on the continuing creation-evolution debate. It is for many, especially students, a troublesome issue fraught with considerable confusion and emotion. I do not believe it has to be that way. In Chapter III, I discussed differences between education—including the sciences—and religion, as well as their compatibility. As an educator, a behavioral scientist, and one of spiritual commitment, I am grateful for the significant contributions of both education and religion.

The creation-evolution issue continues to be a vexing issue. I believe that "In the beginning, God created . . . ." I acknowledge the reality of change and evolution of some forms of life as a process; however, God, a living God, continues to be the prime mover in these processes according to His own agenda and His own timetable. The creation account in Genesis in the Bible is a magnificent briefing of creation which—as with many forms of expression such as the written word in prose and poetry, music, painting, and sculpture—<u>report</u>, <u>uphold</u>, and <u>dignify</u> significant events and moments of human existence. Of all creatures, only human beings have the endowed capacities—mentally, emotionally, and spiritually—to recognize, to experience, and to communicate the truly monumental developments in the history of humankind, such as creation.

Although Darwinism is but a theory, it is built into some school curricula and oftentimes taught as fact. On the other hand, creationism is not accorded the same opportunity. It, too, should be taught as the profound statement and reality it is. Provision should be made for presentation and orientation to creationism <u>for all students with the same measure of respect and emphasis with which evolution is taught</u>, underscoring that creation of humankind was originally, and continues to be an act of God, in the image of God, and with the potential of abundant life for people as sons and daughters of God.

Many students have not learned at home or in their schools of God's creation of the universe and that <u>God's act of creating humankind is more—much more—than the creation of physical bodies and existence</u> as experienced by non-human creatures. Men and women are possessed of sharp minds, sensitive hearts, spiritual qualities, and souls with capacities to love others, to do good, to create great music, poetry, and art, and to build a way of life that dignifies and enriches living!

My undergraduate majors were in English and theater arts with minors in the biological sciences and mathematics. My interests throughout my life have been in both the humanities, including music, art, theater, literature, and history, and in the sciences, including the behavioral, biological, and physical sciences. I have served as an arts and sciences dean, and my WWII service was in naval radar. I respect and accept the truth of proven scientific findings through the centuries. I also accept as truth many of the findings learned and expressed by poets, philosophers, and religious leaders as the result of their harnessing the creative dimensions of mind and spirit through study, meditation, and prayer.

In my study of English literature, I became acquainted with the writing of Robert Browning, a 19th century poet. In these times of America's values decline, I especially like his words and his expression of hope in the poem entitled, "Pippo's Song." He wrote:

> The year's at the spring
> And day's at the morn;
> Morning's at seven;

The hillside's dew-pearled;
The lark's on the wing;
The snail's on the thorn;
God's in his heaven -
All's right with the world! (133).

The Apostle Paul urged:

Finally, brethren, whatsoever things are true, whatsoever things are honest, whatsoever things are just,
whatsoever things are pure, whatsoever things are
lovely, whatsoever things are of good report; if
there be any virtue, and if there be any praise, think
on these things. Those things, which ye have both
learned, and received, and heard, and seen in me, do:
and the God of peace shall be with you (Philippians
4:8-9).

He also admonished:

Hold fast that which is good (I Thessalonians 5:21).

These are dimensions of human life, as ordained by God,
which are not experienced by the creatures over which mankind
has dominion.

There are so many other evidences each day of God's creative
power at work among us. The healing of body and mind following
an illness or accident speaks of God's continuing creation. As we
view the predictability and the magnificence of the changing sea-
sons, we are reminded that in the beginning such had to be the
work of a Supreme Being. Likewise, as we note order in the universe—the order of the sun, the moon, the stars, and the plan-
ets—we must accept that such is the result of intelligent design
by a Supreme Being. The role of the tides in preserving order and
stability in the physical world certainly confirms the involvement
of a Supreme Being in creation, and that the marvels of creation
continue.

In the busy, highly competitive world into which we were born, in which we live, and in which—unless changes are made—we will die, most of us are primarily concerned with getting ahead and experiencing material success, a life which for so many does not allow time for the study, prayer, and contemplation that can open doors of spiritual truth. All of this, of course, is relevant in the writing of *The Best of Mind and Spirit*. It is relevant to the frequently stated belief of the author that <u>education</u> and <u>religion</u> are the two most powerful influences in the shaping of both people and nations.

As I write this concluding chapter, it is the Christmas season. For Christians the world over, it is a time of celebration of the birth and life of Jesus foretold in the Old Testament of the Bible and acknowledged in the New Testament to be the Savior. He has been glorified in such works as George Frederick Handel's magnificent oratorio, "The Messiah," Michelangelo's paintings and sculpture, and an abundance of poetry, literature, art, and music. As born of the Virgin Mary and adored and worshipped by Christians everywhere for some 2000 years, we have in the birth and life of Jesus evidence of God's love and His continuing creation. Such is also true of the crucifixion and resurrection of Jesus—the act of a living, creating God who literally gave His Son out of love for humankind as the propitiation for mankind's sins.

Jesus often reminded people, "Ye must be born again" (John 3:7). Those who have departed from God's ways and standards can, through God's grace and with His help, discard the "old self" and be reborn into newness of life. The same opportunity is available and possible for nations that have turned away from God. America, at this time, is in need of a rebirth—and can experience such!

Robert Schuller, who heads The Crystal Cathedral Ministry in Garden Grove, California, wrote as follows in the September 1997 issue of the *American Legion Magazine* (134):

> For nearly 50 years now, I've been a pastor, and I've seen the changes that have come about in people when they allow God to come into their lives.

People of poverty become people of substance and deep character. People of depression and hopelessness become people of courage and hope. People of despair become people of joy. God makes the difference in people's lives. They are transformed! That is why Americans are turning to religion today. They see the evidence. They know their need and the needs of people around them. The only standard that remains true is God. America is turning to God.

Could it be that a rebirth of America is already underway? <u>It may be</u>—and certainly <u>it will be</u>, if we (as Jesus advised us) "Seek ye first the Kingdom of God and His righteousness; <u>and, all these things shall be added unto you</u>" (Matthew 6:33).

Make no mistake about it! God continues to create; and in response to Jesus' prayer, "Thy Kingdom come, Thy will be done on earth, as it is in heaven" (Matthew 6:10), we can know with certainty that <u>if we but seek His help</u>, the present decline in our nation's moral and spiritual values will be reversed, in spite of the contrary efforts of some of us!

Earlier in *The Best of Mind and Spirit*, I quoted from a volume entitled *Choose Life* (11), authored by Rabbi Bernard Mandelbaum. At this point, I quote from another book entitled *Choose Life* (135)[z], co-authored by Arnold Toynbee, an English Protestant historian and educator, and Daisaku Ikeda, a Japanese Buddhist educator. The two authors engaged in lengthy dialogue, which was edited by Richard L. Gage and published as *Choose Life* by the Oxford University Press of the United Kingdom.

Included on the title page of *Choose Life* (135) is the following scripture:

Choose life and then you and your descendants shall live (Deuteronomy 30:19).

Also, in *Choose Life* (135), Toynbee observes:

I hold that the goal of education ought to be religious, not mercenary. Education ought to be a search for an understanding of the meaning and the purpose of life and for discovering the right way to live (135), (p. 61).

Epilogue

I close with two prayers. The first is from an address, "The Battle for Peace," by Conrad N. Hilton, a prominent American businessman who included the ownership and operation of Chicago's Hilton Hotel among his many enterprises. He concluded the address with a prayer entitled, "America on its Knees," offered in another time of crisis in our nation, when worldwide communism was experiencing its greatest influence and power.

The prayer was highly publicized; and an autographed copy was made available to all that requested such. I received a copy and framed it. For more than half a century it has hung in my office(s) at Drake University, Texas A&M University, and Oklahoma State University.

The prayer follows:

> * * * *not beaten there by the hammer & sickle, but* FREELY, INTELLIGENTLY, RESPONSIBLY, CONFIDENTLY, POWERFULLY. *America now knows it can destroy communism & win the battle for peace. We need fear nothing or no one . . . except GOD.*
>
> OUR FATHER IN HEAVEN:
>
> WE PRAY that YOU save us from *ourselves.*
>
> The world that YOU have made for us, to live in peace,
>   We live in fear of war to come.
> We are afraid of "the terror that flies by
>   night, and the arrow that flies by day,
>   the pestilence that walks in darkness
>   and the destruction that wastes at noon-day."

We have turned from YOU to go our selfish way.
We have broken YOUR commandments
and denied YOUR truth. We have left YOUR altars
to serve the false gods of money and pleasure and power.

FORGIVE US AND HELP US.

Now, darkness gathers around us and we are confused
in all our counsels. Losing faith in YOU,
we lose faith in ourselves.
Inspire us with wisdom, all of us of every color, race and creed,
to use our wealth, our strength to help our brother,
instead of destroying him.

Help us to do YOUR will as it is done in heaven
and to be worthy of YOUR promise of peace on earth.

Fill us with new faith, new strength and new courage,
that we may win the Battle for Peace.

Be swift to save us, *dear God*,
before the darkness falls * * *

The second prayer is the Lord's Prayer. When Jesus' disciples asked him "how to pray," He gave them what is known as "The Lord's Prayer," regarded by untold millions of the world's peoples as the most universal, profound, and relevant prayer ever uttered. It is a prayer of praise and adoration of God, a prayer for sustenance, a prayer for forgiveness, a prayer for deliverance from temptation and evil.

Our Father which art in heaven,
Hallowed be thy name.
Thy Kingdom come.
Thy will be done on earth, as it is in heaven.
Give us this day our daily bread.
And forgive us our debts, as we forgive our debtors.
And lead us not into temptation, but deliver us
from evil:

For thine is the kingdom, and the power,
and the glory forever.
Ämen (Matthew 6:9-13).

Acknowledgments

This volume is written because of:

<u>My love of family</u>—My best friend and wife of more than 58 years, Maxine; our dear parents; our daughter Susan, her husband Phillip White, and their son, Jeffrey; our son Steve, his wife Peggy, their two sons, Derek and Clayton, and their daughter Jessica; and our brothers and sisters.

<u>My love of people generally</u>—My teachers, mentors, pastors, students, and colleagues through the years, both from America and from other nations of the world.

<u>My love of America and its citizens</u>—Of what America has been morally and spiritually, and what it can become again.

<u>My love of God</u>—the Supreme Being of the universe, the living God of love, justice, and goodness.

I am grateful to those who critiqued the preliminary copy of *The Best of Mind and Spirit* and who offered counsel and suggestions. They are my distinguished friends and colleagues from the Oklahoma State University faculty and staff: Dr. LeRoy Fischer, Oppenheimer Professor of History Emeritus; Dr. Kevin Hayes, Professor and Director of Agricultural Communications Services; Mr. Lynn Hazelbaker, Supervisor, Computer Aided Drafting and Design, and translator to modern English of John Bunyan's *The Pilgrim's Progress*; and Dr. Kyle Yates, long-time holder of the Phoebe Schertz Young Chair in Religion, and Head of the Department of Religious Studies, Emeritus.

I very much appreciate Dr. Larry Hynson for his thoughtful

and insightful Foreword to *The Best of Mind and Spirit* and Mr. Gary Hellman, Area Director, Christian Ministries, Campus Crusade for Christ (Oklahoma and Arkansas) for his interest and support.

I thank Dean Ann Candler Lotven of the College of Education, Oklahoma State University, for her thoughtful review and comments of Chapters VII and VIII.

The work of Diane LaFollette, Secretary in the Emeriti Presidents Office, has been invaluable. She not only typed copy, but also made many helpful suggestions along the way. She was much more than a typist. Like the others who assisted, she is a much appreciated colleague.

I am most grateful for the kind words and support of those who have written endorsements of *The Best of Mind and Spirit*: Mr. Patrick McGuigan, Editor of the Editorial Page of *The Daily Oklahoman*, Oklahoma City, Oklahoma; Dr. Floyd Coppedge, Secretary of Education, State of Oklahoma; Dr. Bill Bright, President and Co-Founder of Campus Crusade for Christ International, Orlando, Florida; Dr. Norbert Mahnken, Emeritus Professor of History, Oklahoma State University, Stillwater, Oklahoma; Mr. Russell Heater, Director for UNESCO Affairs, Department of State, 1975-78, Springfield, Virginia; Superintendent Sandy Garrett, Oklahoma State Department of Education, Oklahoma City, Oklahoma; and Dr. Mouzon Biggs, Jr., Sr. Minister, The Boston Avenue Church, United Methodist, Tulsa, Oklahoma.

Additionally, I appreciate other friends and colleagues who have assisted me in special ways in my professional life, including the production of *The Best of Mind and Spirit*. They are former U.S. Senator Henry Bellmon, Dr. John Crooch, Dr. Bob Hamm, Dr. Tom Karman, Dr. Mel Jones, Mr. Forrest McIntire, Dr. Harold Sare, Mr. Dail West and Dr. Oliver Willham.

Finally, two people to whom I am much indebted are Mr. Louis Kramp, a good friend of some 40 years and currently consultant to government groups in Washington, D.C., and Mr. Dale Crawshaw of the Wisdom Press in Cumming, Georgia, a good friend and publisher of *The Best of Mind and Spirit.*

Initially, a copy of the book was shared with Mr. Kramp. He liked it and generously shared it with some prospective publishers, including Mr. Crawshaw, who also liked the book. Subsequently, a contract was signed for Wisdom Press to publish *The Best of Mind and Spirit.*

About the Author

Robert B. Kamm is President Emeritus and Professor Emeritus of the Oklahoma State University. A WWII veteran in Naval radar, he is a product of public education in America, with a Ph.D. in counseling psychology and higher education from the University of Minnesota in 1948. He is a Distinguished Member of the National Honor Society of Phi Kappa Phi and was named a Fellow in the Division of Counseling Psychology of the American Psychological Association in 1954.

Active at local, state, regional and national levels in Church, YMCA, Scouting, and other community programs, he served with ambassador rank in 1976 and 1977 as the USA member of the Executive Board of the United Nations Educational, Scientific, and Cultural Organization, headquartered in Paris, France. In November and December of 1976, he served as chairman of the USA delegation to UNESCO's World Conference in Nairobi, Kenya. His professional travels and service have taken him to some 50 different nations of the world.

In 1978, he was the Republican nominee, State of Oklahoma, for the United States Senate. From 1982-1992, he directed Oklahoma State University's 26-volume Centennial Histories Project, which was recognized by the American Association of State and Local History with its highest honor, the Award of Merit. He has authored five books and 72 journal articles. He served as president of the American College Personnel Association in 1957-58, and is a former chairman of the Council of Presidents of the National Association of State Universities and Land-Grant Colleges. He has been listed in *Who's Who in America* since 1955, and later was named to *Who's Who in the World*. He is also listed in *Who's Who in American Education* and *American Men of Science*. In 1976, he was named "Oklahoman of the Year" by the Oklahoma Broadcasters Association. Of an informal nature, he was honored to serve in 1996 as an Olympic Torchbearer.

In addition to the preceding listing of information about the author, it is of note that his emphasis on <u>both</u> <u>mind</u> <u>and</u> <u>spirit</u> (as expressed in *The Best of Mind and Spirit*) has been a <u>dominant</u> <u>concern</u> of his for most of his life—as a student, a teacher, an education administrator, and a citizen locally, nationally, and internationally.

Appendices C, D, E, F, and G which follow, contain thoughts expressed in some of his earlier publications. Actually, *The Best of Mind and Spirit* is the culmination of a lifetime of emphasis on both <u>mind</u> and <u>spirit</u>.

The Need for Talent in All Worthwhile Labor

(136)

Robert B. Kamm, Dean
College of Arts and Sciences
The Oklahoma State University

(with emphasis on the dignity of all
worthwhile labor done well)

"Rich man, poor man, beggar man, thief—
Doctor, lawyer, merchant, chief . . ."

. . . and so goes the familiar nursery rhyme.

Ours is indeed a complex and diverse society. It is a society of many different activities and of many different needs to be served. It is a society of individuals, of people with varying talents and abilities. Certainly, the nursery rhyme just cited suggests some of society's needs and problems, as well as some of the vocations necessary to serve the needs of mankind.

How does one choose an appropriate vocation in today's complex world and in this time of rapid change? Many considerations enter into the making of an intelligent career decision. Primarily, a thorough understanding of one's abilities and knowledge of the needs of society are important. To be more specific, there is need to recognize that each of us is an <u>individual</u>, uniquely endowed to serve in a way no one else can serve. In a day in which there is considerable public pressure for young people to choose this vocation or that, the task of counseling (by parents, teachers, and counselors) must be one of helping students come to know their unique abilities and then to suggest (if such seems in order) a number of possible alternative vocations in which the person might live and work with genuine personal satisfaction in service to others and in harmony with his/her highest spiritual goals and commitments.

It should be emphasized that a vocational decision should always be made by the individual concerned, not by a parent, friend, or counselor. No one of us, regardless of the extent of our education and experience or of the extent of interest we have in another person, is in a position to actually know what vocation is the best one for someone else. At best, we can only help others better understand themselves and to point out possible career alternatives for their study.

Sometimes high school students (because of wrong counsel or because of pressures of the home or of the public) make career choices too early, with the result that there are frustrations in college and a lifetime of job unhappiness. Especially in the world of rapid change in which we now live, it seems wise that the choice of a career be deferred as long as possible. Recognizing that it is necessary for some young people to decide on a vocation by the time of high school graduation, it is recognized, too, that for most it is unnecessary to do so until after a year or two of college, during which time the student will have had opportunity to become better acquainted with his/her own abilities and with the world of work. It should be emphasized that the making of a vocational decision is a <u>process</u>, not an event. Several years of study and evaluation may be necessary in some cases before an appropriate career decision can be made.

In making a vocational choice, it should also be noted that, increasingly, the world of work is recognizing the need for broadly educated people. Medicine, teaching, engineering, law, business, and the ministry (to mention but some areas) are requiring increasing amounts of broad, liberal education. Recognizing that today's students must be prepared to live and work in the world of tomorrow (in which many of today's jobs will no longer exist and new ones will have been developed), the emphasis, more and more, is on breadth learning. Accordingly, to defer the making of a specific vocational choice for an additional year or two (during which time emphasis can be placed on learning more of one's abilities as well as on achieving breadth in educational programs) appears to be sound from the standpoint of good guidance.

What are the vocational opportunities that exist today? Accepting the fact that it is necessary, first of all, for each individual to assess carefully his/her own strengths and weaknesses and to then relate such to the work needs of society, what are some fields of endeavor which might be considered by young people in these modern times?

We live today in what some term a "technical society"—an age in which science and the applications of science abound. Billions of dollars in this Nation are being spent annually in scientific research and endeavor. Such United States government agencies as the National Science Foundation, the National Institutes of Health and the National Aeronautical and Space Administration are giving great impetus to science and technology.

Today's society needs scientists—scientists of all manners and kinds; those who deal in the realms of theory and discovery and those who apply scientific knowledge.

Biological scientists are needed—botanists, entomologists, microbiologists, geneticists, physiologists, and zoologists, and others. Necessary, too, are those who apply knowledge in the biological sciences including medical doctors, dentists, nurses, medical technologists, space physiologists, veterinarians, dairymen, foresters, agronomists, food and nutrition experts, aquatic biologists, and wildlife conservationists.

Physical scientists are needed, including chemists, geologists, physicists, astronomers, and meteorologists. Also, those who apply the physical sciences are needed including engineers and space scientists.

Mathematicians, statisticians, and high-speed computing personnel—these, too, are needed in great numbers today. Add the need for technicians in the various scientific and engineering fields and one becomes all the more aware of the fact that ours is, to a rather great extent, an "age of science."

But ours is more than a scientific and technical society, important as these are. Many activities contribute to the whole of life in 21st Century America and of the World. Many functions and needs must be served; and varied talents and competencies are needed.

We need many more outstanding teachers and counselors, for an informed populace is basic to the preservation of freedom. We need to point out to great numbers of talented young men and women the challenges and rewards of the teaching profession. In addition, we need to make the profession so attractive that many will choose to make education a life-long career.

We need able young men and women in government service—locally, nationally, and internationally. Certainly, fine minds are needed in all areas of law and political endeavor as well as in the communications media such as journalism and radio/television. Top historians, economists, accountants, and management personnel are needed, as are able fashion designers, architects, and businessmen.

Many are needed in the great fields of social service. Teaching and counseling have already been mentioned. The areas of sociology, social work, and psychology are rapidly growing fields. Also, we need those who know well the geography of the world, as well as its different peoples and cultures.

Theology and the ministry need great numbers of additional personnel—young men and women of the highest ability levels—to guide and to lead in the making of right decisions in the use of the abundance of knowledge which is ours today.

Creative endeavor and artistic activity of all kinds need to be encouraged in today's world of increasing leisure-time—and those with special talents should be identified early and encouraged in the development of their unique abilities. Increasing numbers of those with talent in music, the theater, painting, sculpture, writing, the dance, health, physical education, and recreation are needed today.

Many more vocational opportunities might be named. Certainly, mention should be made of our significant roles as parents, homemakers, and citizens. Again, the importance and value of breadth of education should be noted. Suffice it to say, in concluding this statement that at the very foundation of the process of vocational guidance must be <u>concern for the individual</u>. The welfare of individuals and of a society comprised of individuals must take precedence over all other considerations in the making of a vocational choice. This is <u>freedom</u>—freedom to become the best for which each of us is uniquely qualified, rather than to be misled or forced into work which is not consistent with our highest abilities and aspirations.

Our Vocation Is Students

(137)

Robert B. Kamm, Dean
College of Arts and Sciences
Oklahoma State University

(with emphasis on the spiritual
dimension of our labors)

Since it is to the subject of vocation that we direct our attention today, perhaps we might best begin by looking at the definition of the word itself. Webster speaks of vocation as: (a) a calling to a particular state, business, or profession; (b) regular or appropriate employment; and (c) a calling to the service of God in a particular station or state of life. The first two definitions have clear meaning, so far as the vocational guidance movement is concerned. It is in the interests of "appropriate employment" of individuals that our vocational guidance agencies operate. This, in a nutshell, is the "why" of vocational guidance, so far as most guidance personnel are concerned. For the thoughtful religious person, however, this is only part of the story. We who have grown up in the Hebraic-Christian tradition of America—most of us in the Christian faith—should also be cognizant of the theological implications of the term. If our religious convictions have meaning for our lives beyond an hour each Sunday morning, if our beliefs are of real depth, then there must be carry-over of them into our work-a-day lives.

Dr. Carl Michalson, professor of Systematic Theology at the Theological School, Drew University, discussed "the crisis of vocation" in a recent work (141). He takes note of the importance of work to all of us. He discusses at some length the pressures and anxieties, the self-torture and aimlessness that characterize so much of our vocational life—the "pathology of vocational life." He explains the New Testament use of the word vocation as a calling to salvation, and states, further, that "a man's life of faith is not suspended during working hours," that one's vocational life is actually the arena in which God's calling is worked out.

How do we conceive of our roles? What are the dimensions of vocation, so far as we are concerned? Is it a mere job in which each of us is engaged?

I submit, concerned as we are with the total and proper development of young men and women, that ours is a far loftier role than can be contained in any purely secular category of "worker." Our vocation is students! We who are educators and student personnel workers, if we are to carry out properly the many duties and responsibilities that are ours, must view our efforts in the light of the theological implications of vocation. To do less is to fall short of our high calling.

One immediately encounters the notion on many of our campuses that, so far as religion is concerned, we must be neutral. Such a position is erroneous. We are free, both at our private and at our public institutions, to bring the religious dimension to our work. On our church-related campuses, the task may be somewhat easier because of acknowledged religiously oriented purposes and goals of the institution. At our public institutions the problems are undoubtedly greater, although if on our publicly supported campuses we provide genuine freedom for all faith groups to operate and to flourish, no real problem need exist. So often, however, instead of encouraging each faith group to carry on in its fullest and best tradition, we have (more or less) "put the lid" on religious groups.

Let us, first of all, look at certain historical aspects of the situation. In the early days of American higher education, the church was chiefly responsible for and involved in the development of colleges and universities. During the last half of the nineteenth century and well into the twentieth century, there appears to have been somewhat of a drifting apart of religion and education. The belief that religion was the concern of other agencies of society gained considerable impetus. This period marked the beginning of great emphasis on scientific development, of the "scientific pursuit of truth." Certain supposed conflicts between science and religion to which we in our present state of greater maturity hardly give a second thought, received considerable attention and served to emphasize the seeming incompatibility between education and religion.

In recent years, however, there seems to be a growing realization of the compatibility of education and religion. Kenneth I. Brown, in his volume *Not Minds Alone* (142), lists as examples of higher education's great interest in religion, the activities of the National Council on Religion in Higher Education, the Edward W. Hazen Foundation, the Danforth Foundation, the Commission on Christian Education of the Association of American Colleges, the Educational Policies Commission of the National Education Association, and the Committee on Religion in Education of the American Council on Education. Also, as evidence, he cites the organization of the Faculty Christian Fellowship, as well as the abundance of recent literature dealing with religion in education, including such volumes as Sir Walter Moberly's *The Crisis in the University* (143) and Howard Lowry's *The Mind's Adventure* (144).

Why the pulling apart of education and religion experienced in the second period and continuing even today? What has contributed to the separation of the two? Several considerations entered in.

The first of these major influences, as far as our state and public institutions are concerned, is the principle of "separation of church and state." Yet the separation of church and state refers to separation of control only. Never was it intended by this nation's founders that the state or any of its parts in any way adopt a hands-off policy with regard to religion. Quite the contrary, in fact. Norman Cousins, in his book *In God We Trust* (145), presents the religious beliefs of the men who founded the United States—Benjamin Franklin, George Washington, Thomas Jefferson, John Adams, Samuel Adams, James Madison, Alexander Hamilton, John Jay, and Thomas Paine. Differing in their beliefs, to be sure, they nevertheless recognized the need and wisdom of acknowledging God in the important tasks that were theirs.

Merrimon Cuninggim, in his volume *The College Seeks Religion* (146), observes that John Dewey and others have stated that the American tradition argues against any connection of religion and state. Cuninggim points out that the evidence is overwhelmingly against this thinking when one considers the wording of the Declaration of Independence and other official documents, Thanksgiving Day proclamations, the use of prayer in legislative bodies, the presence of chaplains in the Armed Forces, and the ascription in state and federal courts that certain elements of religious faith are part of the common law of the land. He states further:

> There does not exist any nationwide legal or constitutional principle which prevents such institutions [tax supported] from including religion in their programs, if they so desire. Their own state laws or court interpretations may raise difficulties. These occur in only a small minority of the states, and there is no state in which nothing at all can be done (146).

Separation of church and state, interpreted in terms of separation of <u>control of one by the other</u>, is good and absolutely necessary. To interpret the concept of separation as denying the youth who attend our public institutions the opportunity to mature spiritually as a part of their over-all development is completely erroneous and without foundation.

Certainly, a second major contributor to the lessened influence of religion in educational programs has been the bickering and the failure to resolve differences by church groups themselves. In many ways, the various denominational groups have been their own worst enemies so far as the cause of religion in higher education is concerned. Kenneth I. Brown (142) points out:

> A century or less ago, if the churches in America had been able to agree on the deserved place of religion, and particularly the kind of religion, in the public schools, we would not today be faced with the censored education which is our portion. The contemporary patterns of religionless education are the work of a disagreeing Christianity more than a proselyting secularism.

A third contributor has been that of the rather commonly held distrust of religion by some educators, a fear that with religious commitment comes limitation on free inquiry. To be sure, some of our denominational groups have balked at free inquiry, and perhaps therein rests some of the cause for the dichotomy of education and religion that exists.

It is fair to say, I believe, that most church groups today, as in the early years, support the development of scholarship and free inquiry. Dr. Robert Calhoun, professor of Historical Theology, Yale Divinity School (147), states:

> Religion needs the constant association with intellectual discipline and liberating insight, . . . comparison with known fact, . . . and the critical temper of fine-edged minds constantly at work to keep its perspective clear.

Sir Richard Livingstone, Vice Chancellor of the University of Oxford, has proposed that some study of religion or philosophy, or both, should be included in all undergraduate courses (148) so that the college or university will send out into the world men (sic) equipped not merely to use and improve the means of life, but to direct and inspire its ends and to be instruments in its regeneration. Sir Walter Moberly likewise emphasized the importance of religion in determining the ends for which scientific knowledge should be used (143).

The religious dimension can and must be a part of our daily work as educators, whether we be teachers, counselors, or administrators. Whether we serve in a church-related institution where we may speak out in the fullest traditions of the sponsoring faith; or whether we serve in a public institution where each of us, although not at liberty to indoctrinate, is nevertheless completely free to witness to our own beliefs; we must take cognizance of the high role of religion.

Much, I submit, depends upon the concept of vocation that we have. This is a time of national emergency, of a different kind, to be sure, than that which we ordinarily read about, but even more devastating. We are today confronted with forces of materialism, absence of purpose, and moral laxness within our borders that can cause our downfall just as surely as attack from outside forces!

Our responsibilities are indeed great! How can we measure up to them? Is vocation defined as "regular or appropriate employment" sufficient to the demands of the times in which we live? Sufficient for the full and proper development of the students whom we serve? Sufficient for our own self-fulfillment? I think not. Ours is no ordinary job. Ours is a much higher role than that of mere employment. Our vocation is students. Only a definition of vocation that recognizes us as images of God responsible to Him and the beneficiaries of His love, engaged in the service of others of His children, is big enough to contain the high calling which is ours.

Restoration in Discipline

(138)

Robert B. Kamm
Dean of Students
Drake University

(with emphasis on rehabilitation in discipline)

College and university student personnel programs vary great-ly, both in terms of type of organization and in extent of servic-es offered. Some institutions assume little responsibility for out-of-class activities of students, whereas others provide extensive services aimed at aiding in the full maturation of students—mentally, physically, socially, and spiritually. It is their belief that the educational program of a college or university consists of both instructional services and student personnel services. This point of view, commonly spoken of as "the student personnel point of view," is well presented in an American Council On Education brochure entitled *The Student Personnel Point of View* (149). Along with a statement of philosophy and a discussion of basic needs of college students, a comprehensive listing of rec-ommended student personnel services is presented.

As mentioned, there is widespread practice in higher educa-tion today to provide help in as many need areas as is possible, although some institutions (possibly because of budgetary restric-tion or because of the educational philosophy of those responsi-ble for its operation) still provide limited services. It is probable, however, that a common denominator of all institutions is the student personnel responsibility for student conduct and discipline. Although the degree of responsibility assumed may again vary from college to college, it is doubtful if many institutions, if any, overlook the matter of the behavior of their students. If nothing more, the concern (in the event of undesirable student conduct) may be only a selfish one of public relations—"to take an appropriate action" to demonstrate to the college's clientele that it will not tolerate this or that wrong!

To be sure, there are some students who are unable to profit from the college experience, even with competent and sympathetic help. When such is the case, or when the continued presence of an offender threatens the welfare of fellow students and the institution, it may be necessary to separate that student from the college or university. It must be recognized that institutions of higher education are established for service to a rather limited segment of society. Extreme deviates and those otherwise incapable of benefiting from the college experience must be served by other types of institutions specifically geared to their needs.

And yet, recognizing the above facts, a program that aims at rehabilitation of offenders (and even in the case of those who cannot be permitted to continue at an institution, aims at aiding them in gaining insight relative to their problems and to the appropriateness of the dismissal action) is education in its richest sense. Such a concept of education is in complete harmony with the student personnel point of view—a point of view that recognizes that the center of all educational attentions is the individual student, and that his welfare and proper development are of paramount concern. It does not "buy" the concept that "the punishment must fit the crime." Rather it states that discipline is an educational process—that effective discipline aims at rehabilitation of an offender.

Hawkes and Hawkes, in their chapter on Discipline in *Through a Dean's Open Door* (150), stress, "Whether it be academic failure or moral failure or social failure, the responsibility of the college is the same—to educate, not to punish. It stands to reason that education must be adapted to the needs of the individual being educated."

In both *Through a Dean's Open Door* and in a later writing of Mrs. Hawkes in a chapter of the volume *Student Personnel Work as Deeper Teaching* (151) edited by Lloyd-Jones and Smith, it is emphasized that "a college is an educational institution, educational not only in the domain of the mind, but also in the realm of the spirit."

Wrenn, in *Student Personnel Work in College* (152), points out that "a discipline program should attempt to <u>prevent</u> conditions that cause delinquent behavior, and the <u>learning values</u> of the situation for the student should be given first consideration."

Williamson and Foley, in their book *Counseling and Discipline* (153), state ". . . the main purpose of disciplinary counseling is to alleviate the cause of misbehavior so that these causes will no longer operate, so that <u>it will no longer be necessary for the student to offend society. The purpose is to cure, and not to punish</u>. The student who gets into difficulties of one sort or another is treated as an individual who needs special teaching assistance, and the whole process is organized to take account of the student's assets and liabilities and thus to effect his rehabilitation within the limits of his potentialities."

Occasionally in one's experience, there are happenings that "out of the clear" serve to reinforce or to give new meaning and vitality to a point of view. Such was true of the writer recently, so far as his philosophy of discipline is concerned, in the reading of Alan Paton's best-seller, *Too Late the Phalarope* (154). In this moving presentation of the struggle within a man of right and wrong, the phalarope, a beautiful, rarely-observed bird of South Africa, is symbolic of the love we so often fail to give those who really mean the most to us.

Pieter van Vlaanderen, a deeply conscientious young Boer police lieutenant, a rugby star, and a war hero, harbors within himself tensions and conflicts which are heightened because of failure to communicate with, and to gain understanding of those closest to him—including a narrow, austere father and a naïve wife who is unable to comprehend and to share in the deep longings, needs, and desires of her husband.

Pieter eventually succumbs to evil and violates the Immorality Act of South Africa, an act governing the relationship between black and white.

Some time after Pieter's confession to his police captain who recognizes the severity of the penalty which will follow, the captain and Pieter's aunt (who has been denied access to her brother's home as the result of choosing to remain loyal to her nephew in his time of need rather than to forever disown him, as Pieter's father had done) walk silently in the captain's home. Finally, the captain, deeply disturbed and moved by what has happened, comments, "An offender must be punished . . . I don't argue about that. But to punish and not to restore, that is the greatest of all offenses."

Later, in relating to Pieter's unforgiving father-in-law what has happened, the captain repeats, "If man takes unto himself God's right to punish, then he must also take upon himself God's promise to restore."

These words from *Too Late the Phalarope* give new body and freshness to the concept in discipline of rehabilitation. Coming from one who is not directly associated with student personnel work, these statements give added vitality and zest to a point of view generally subscribed to by those working in the field. They challenge us anew to bear in mind always that the welfare and proper development of individual students is paramount.

The Management of Conflict
(139)

Robert B. Kamm
President, Oklahoma State University
Member-at-Large, The General Council,
Omicron Delta Kappa National Leadership Fraternity

(with emphasis on love, respect, and goodwill)

I wish to share with you today some thoughts relative to the management of conflict. Tension, frustration, and conflict are all about us. They are so much parts of life in these days in which we live. We must learn to live with conflict if we are to survive as individuals; and, those of us with management responsibilities have got to learn to deal effectively with conflict, if we are to do our jobs successfully.

Someone has observed that if anyone has the qualifications to speak on managing conflict, it is a university president! It is true that campuses in recent years have been arenas of unrest and conflict to a degree never experienced before.

Youth have always been idealistic (thank goodness!)—and campuses are places where great numbers of youth reside, usually in a high-density relationship. Add in such considerations as the following, and some of the recent happenings on campuses can be better understood:

1. The undeclared, costly, and much-misunderstood Vietnam War;

2. Civil rights issues, as those who have been denied their rights for so long seek opportunities to achieve dignity and to realize their full potential;

3. The economic affluence of recent decades. (With an abundance of material resources, many young people have been denied certain opportunities to achieve for themselves. Accordingly, other means to achieve self-fulfillment have been devised, some of which have differed greatly from traditional acceptable behavior);

4. The sometimes-poor example set by the parental generation, as they have striven to succeed in life. (To be sure, great good has come from this generation, as well as from earlier generations; but there are many evidences, too, of insensitivity to the impact of their lifestyles on others);

5. The quality of life issue;

6. The technological revolution, with its all-too-frequent greater emphasis on things than on people.

More such considerations might be mentioned, but the preceding serve to explain in part at least, the "more than usual" tension and conflict on campuses the past decade.

Many people ask me why I'm a university president. Well, it's because I enjoy being a president! When I cease to enjoy such, I'll quietly bow out. To be sure it is a job of both great pleasures and great pressures. So far the pleasures have outweighed the pressures.

Someone has likened the role of university presidents to that of a couple of mice in the nose cone of a rocket headed for the moon. The mice were discussing their situation and one observed, "Well, at least this beats cancer research!"

A president was quitting, and a friend asked, "Why?" The president replied, "I'm sick and tired of the abuse. As but one example, I'm tired of people saying 'shoot college presidents and barbers.'" There was a pause and then the friend asked, "Why barbers?" At this point the president threw his hands in the air and observed, "That's just my point! That's what everyone asks."

Let me now share with you some thoughts that have meaning

for me in dealing with conflict situations. I have a Ph.D. in Psychology, and I considered giving a talk on some such subject as "Role Theory of Social Systems," or "Role Conflict." I decided the worst thing I could do, however, would be to attempt to show such sophistication in interpersonal relationships, for I would probably immediately be suspect. As many of you know, we've had great emphasis in our graduate training programs in psychology, personnel work, and management, on the science of dealing with our <u>fellow human beings</u>. All too often, we've become known as manipulators of people. We've gone about our job "according to the book," and sometimes we've failed to realize we are working with real people—that we are working with fellow human beings. To be sure, science and technology have contributed much to management theory and practice—and I applaud such. What I wish to underscore today, however, is that dealing with conflict is more an <u>art</u> than it is a <u>science</u>. If college and university administrators have learned anything as the result of the unusual events on campuses in recent years, it is that those earlier lessons learned from their scientifically-oriented graduate level textbooks have had limited meaning for campus confrontation. Some approaches, however, are part of the "art" of managing conflict and have led to an easing of tensions and conflict, to establishing stability on campuses, and to productivity in campus situations.

Perhaps the most important consideration is that <u>we love people</u>. It is the most basic consideration. We have to love people regardless of how unlovely they may be, or how unkind they may be.

Nearly 1600 years ago, St. Augustine answered the question, "What does love look like?" He said:

> It has the hands to help others,
> It has the feet to hasten to the poor and needy.
> It has the eyes to see misery and want.
> It has the ears to hear the sighs and sorrows of men.
> That is what love looks like.

We need to genuinely love others, not only for their happiness and for their maximum productivity, but also for the sake of the survival of the human race! The only way you and I can "stay alive on the vine" and retain our sanity and perspective in the rugged times in which we live, is to nurture love within us. We'll surely die unless we build on love—a love rooted in the love of the God of all mankind—for all people.

Secondly, we need to recognize the centrality of people. If people are not now central in our thoughts and our efforts, then we need to make them central. Great and good things can happen if people know they are important. People who feel little and unwanted will probably perform poorly, regardless of how significant the task is. On the other hand, people who feel accepted and important can accomplish much, even if the task may be humdrum and difficult. I am thinking, for example, of the wonderful lady who takes care of my office. She is doing her job well; and she needs the recognition for a job well done. Expressing a sincere "thank you" now and then, incidentally, can do wonders for both the person being thanked and the one doing the thanking.

Thirdly, and related to the preceding, is the need to respect people for what they are and for what they do in our organizations, regardless of how humble their jobs may be. Through the years, in working with students, I have come to believe in the "every person a leader" concept. I believe that at some time, in some situation, every person can lead, whether a one, two, or five-talented person. Consider a plumber, for example. Certainly he must be acknowledged as "leader," as we look to him to correct a plumbing deficiency.

Well, we must love people; we must recognize the centrality of people; and we must respect people for what they are and for what they do, as we attempt to deal appropriately with conflict.

These are attitudes. They're important. Some other things are important, too. I think, for example, that in dealing with conflict we must make the ground rules of our operation very clear, so that misunderstandings and conflicts can be minimized. Whether it be a matter of student enrollment, or of acceptance by an employee of a position, it helps for the person involved to know what the expectations are of him in the setting of which he'll be a part. These need to be clearly spelled out and, hopefully, understood by all concerned.

Related to this is the <u>need to know the mission of the enterprise</u> by all involved. We live in a time of uncertainty. We must make every effort to minimize uncertainty as to the <u>why</u> of our enterprise as emphasized in stressing the need for communicating ground rules so there can be considerable reduction in the amount of conflict to be managed if the mission of our enterprise is known and understood.

Along with the setting down of certain ground rules and the clear stating of our mission, there is also need <u>to provide for the free traffic of ideas</u>. Thoughtful, responsible sharing of thinking, whether on a campus or in the off-campus world, can result in the lessening of conflict and tension and of the increasing of productivity and progress of our efforts.

This is not a matter of where the ultimate authority resides. It's simply a matter of letting those who share in the enterprise to be sincerely heard. I don't know of anything more important in dealing with conflict than to have people feel they have honestly been listened to.

I would submit also that we need to be more than managers in the arena of conflict. We must also be <u>leaders</u>. To some extent, this entails being an example. Keeping our "cool" in the face of conflict, as example, may help others to keep their "cool."

To a large extent, being a leader also means, "setting the pace" in terms of hard work and long hours. It means coming up with sound ideas that will resolve conflict and reduce tension. It means loving the unlovely and the disagreeable, as previously mentioned, even when we may feel unloved.

It means communicating a "cool," a measure of confidence, a degree of commitment to the cause, even when things may appear bleak, for if those in charge falter in some conflict situations, the whole enterprise may fail.

I would remind you, in closing, that in higher education we're primarily concerned with <u>people</u> rather than with things. Our lives probably would be much less complicated and freer of conflict if we weren't so much involved with our fellow human beings! But our lives would probably not be nearly as interesting or as blessed. The really important achievements in life do not come without conflict or struggle.

A couple of weeks ago, Christians the world over celebrated Easter. Certainly, Christ had a lot to say about dealing with conflict and tension, not only for His day, but also for today and for all times. Certainly, He was not spared the trials and tribulations that accompany dealing with conflict.

We should not expect the load to be light or the job to be easy. To work with our fellow human beings, however, toward the end of resolving problems and reducing tensions and conflicts can be a truly lofty and most worthwhile experience—and I'm glad to be so involved.

The Object of My Affection
(140)

Robert B. Kamm, Professor
Educational Administration and Higher Education
Oklahoma State University

(with emphasis on people)

A half-century ago, Messrs. Pinky Tomlin and Jimmy Grier combined their talents to produce the music and lyrics for a delightful little song entitled "The Object of My Affection." The tune and the words linger, but they have taken on additional meaning for me through the years.

As a participant in the higher education scene for most of the half-century since the song was written, I've had the opportunity to view considerable change in higher education—most for the good, but also some which I question. As an undergraduate in the 1930s, I felt I was very much "the object of their affections," so far as my teachers and counselors were concerned. In fact, I was so impressed with their interest and caring that I made a career decision that I would try to serve students in some special ways. Subsequently, I received a doctorate in educational psychology and served as a dean of students, as a dean of a college of arts and sciences, as an academic vice president, and, for nearly 11 years, as president of a large, comprehensive university. Since leaving the presidency in 1977, I have taught courses in higher education administration. Always, throughout my various involvements in higher education, "the object of my affection" has been the student.

My observations of the higher education scene lead me to believe, however, that there has been considerable decline in recent decades in our commitment to the notion of the centrality of the student in American higher education. Most faculty members of earlier years when asked, "Who, or what is of highest priority in higher education?" would have answered, "The student." Many today would likely reply, "My research;" "My scholarly activity and writing;" "My discipline and/or my professional association;" or "My public service and consulting." Many administrators and staff personnel today, in answer to the same question, would probably say, "Fundraising;" or "My dealings with off-campus publics."

The purpose of this paper is not to minimize the importance of any of the preceding aspects. In fact, at the outset, I would underscore higher education's special and unique mission in society—to preserve, enrich, and transmit our culture through teaching, research, extension, and public service. In modern American higher education there must, of course, be those who devote much of their time and energies to such activities. For example, there is need in comprehensive universities for researchers that literally lose themselves in the excitement and significance of their research. But I would hope they would still maintain some measure of a mentoring relationship with students—usually graduate students who, like undergraduates, also have problems and require nurture. There is need, too, for administrators and other staff personnel who must spend much of their time relating to individuals and groups off the campus. Still, they must recognize that success of off-campus efforts, to a very great extent, relate directly to what's happening on-campus—especially the experiences of students, for their attitudes do impact off-campus relationships.

The purpose of this paper is not to glorify "the golden past." Far from it! We've come so far in so many ways the past 50 years;

and, there is so much that is good in present-day American higher education. It is well to note, also, that there have been many changes during the past half century that make today's campus climate quite different from the one I knew as an undergraduate. In many ways, students themselves are different. They are a much more diverse group; and generally, they are more "on their own" than were their predecessors. They assume certain responsibilities at an earlier age, such as voting at 18 rather than at 21.

One thing has changed little, however—I refer to <u>the continuing need of students for caring and concerned faculty and staff</u>. Whether a newly-enrolled student just beginning college, a middle-aged person picking up his or her studies after years of employment, or a doctoral student preparing for his or her thesis defense, there is need of and appreciation for faculty and staff who are supportive. Some of the most convincing evidence of how important caring faculty and staff are has come in studies of student retention. It is an established fact that the single most important factor in student retention is the expression and practice of care and concern on the parts of faculty and staff.

Let us now proceed to examine possible causes for the decline in attention to students in American higher education. Consider the preoccupation of so many educators today with "making ends meet"—economic survival. Consider change—<u>rapid change</u>—and the attention that must be given to meeting this challenge if institutions are to be instruments for creative change rather than victims of change. Consider conflict on campuses. Although certain conflict is normal and healthy in higher education (e.g., conflict between the old and the new—of new ideas coming out of research and scholarly activity in conflict with previously accepted knowledge) various abnormal conflicts tend to emerge in our present-day, more participative, and more permissive campus climate.

Consider the pressures of a multitude of off-campus groups and forces that vie for the affection of those on the campus. All demand some measure of attention, and all serve to detract from attention to students. There are control (operating) boards to whom the president and his or her staff are accountable for all that goes on at the institution. Then, for state-supported institutions, there has arrived on the scene in recent decades, "coordinating" boards. The additional demands placed on campus personnel by coordinating boards is substantial, adding still further to the competition for the attentions of those charged with operating institutions.

There are various government agencies—local, state, and federal—to which attention must be given. For state colleges and universities, there are governors and legislators with whom to relate. The increased role of the federal government and its agencies in American higher education and the growing encroachment of them on local operations are also evident.

In this time of financial crisis, officials at both public and private institutions have, of necessity, increased their efforts to secure monies from the private sector. Whether it's a matter of just keeping pace financially, or whether it's a matter of economic survival, the involvements of presidents, faculty, and staff in fundraising are increasing, leaving even less time for attention (and affection) to students.

Added to the preceding are the demands and pressures from the various professions with which higher education relates. There are professional societies—more than 80 of them—and they expect attention. Many institutions belong to consortia, and there are obligations and expectations in relation to such. Then there are accrediting agencies and bodies, both special interest in nature (more than 50 of them, such as the National Council for Accreditation of Teacher Education), and general in nature (the regional accrediting bodies). Perhaps no category of outside agencies exceeds accrediting bodies (essential as they are) in demands for the attentions of colleges and universities.

The list of outside agencies and groups that impact higher education goes on and on. There are employment groups—those from all fields of endeavor, who look at our graduates and tell us what we do well or poorly and what we should do differently. There are those of a political and patriotic nature—and they sometimes have special ways of gaining our attention. In the great diversity of American higher education, there are different age groups, nationality groups, and racial groups that demand attention.

There are parents—a group which expected our attention in years past; which for a period in the '60s and '70s seemed to have less to say; but which today is again sharing to a greater extent in the college years of their sons and daughters.

There are alumni and former students—a body of people who, if properly appreciated and nurtured, can be a tremendous asset to an institution. And, there are donors and benefactors. Proper cultivation, direction, and attention to these are essential.

Finally, in this review of outside forces, pressures, and influences on higher education, we need to note such factors as national goals and technological change, the impact of military registration, of war, of space activities, and of the computer. Cultural changes such as the recognition of the equality of the sexes and the need for equal opportunity for all have special meaning for higher education. And there is also our greater involvement internationally, which demands our attention. However manifested—whether in the numbers of students from other lands on our campuses, the numbers of USA students studying abroad, or the numbers of programs abroad in which we share our "know how"—the fact is that we increasingly are becoming "one world;" and we must give even more attention than we have in the past to this reality.

So much for the groups, forces, and influences that compete with students for our attentions. Added to these are the changes in faculty and staff priorities mentioned earlier in this paper, as well as the reduced status, generally, of in loco parentis in American higher education. It is little wonder that many students today are uncertain as to how they rate, so far as the affections of faculty, staff, and administrators are concerned. To be sure, some campuses continue to place a special emphasis on students in the academic enterprise. They are exceptions to the concern just expressed. <u>Generally, however, I do not hesitate to state that substantial numbers of faculty and staff in higher education today fall short in their commitment to students.</u> We're just so busy and occupied with other things that we tend to let students be "on their own." The frequently heard student complaint, "we are just numbers," is probably close to the truth on some campuses. Someone jokingly observed that "the campus would be a great place if it weren't for the students," but it appears there are those in higher education who believe it!

I personally am deeply committed to the notion that students should be the primary "objects of affection" of those of us in higher education. Certainly, as we consider the mission of higher education—to seek for knowledge and to share it—we must also be aware of a companion commitment to students—to serve them well and to assist each to be and to become the best each is capable of being and becoming. An analysis of the mission statements of today's colleges and universities generally serve to reinforce commitment to both academic goals and the development of students.

For nearly 60 years, the American Council on Education has had an active interest in serving the total needs of students. A culmination of years of study and discussion in this area led to the ACE's publication in 1949 of a classic little monograph entitled, *The Student Personnel Point of View.*(aa) It is a document that has meant much to me through the years. I recall, in particular, two statements from the opening page:

> The development of students as whole persons interacting in social situations is the central concern of student personnel work and of other agencies of education;

and

> The student personnel point of view encompasses the student as a whole. The concept of education is

broadened to include attention to the student's well-rounded development—physically, socially, emotionally, and spiritually, as well as intellectually.

These observations continue to be valid and sound, as do hundreds of present-day college and university mission statements that acknowledge commitment to both high academic endeavor and the well-rounded development of students who participate in the higher education experience. Perhaps, however, it is in a discussion of the nature and worth of humankind that we find the most compelling argument for students to be "the objects of our affections." In doing such, we move into the theological realm, with recognition that man is indeed the highest of God's creation. Each individual, whatever his or her talents may be, is of inestimable worth in the eyes of God. Such being the case, how can we possibly relegate the students to a lesser status than other matters that vie for our attention?

To carry the theological dimension a bit further, I like to think that, as educators, our vocation is students. Webster states that vocation is "a calling to a particular state, business, or profession." He also notes that vocation is "regular or appropriate employment." These are the usual and commonly understood definitions of vocation. But Webster has a third definition that states that vocation is "a calling to the service of God in a particular station or state of life." In medieval days this definition was interpreted as applying only to those called to holy orders, but Martin Luther resisted such a limitation and sought to give the term meaning for every person as the situation in which people serve God and others. As educators, I believe our vocation is something more than "regular or appropriate employment." It is more than just a job or a means of making ends meet, important as these are. Serving people as we do, ours is no ordinary role. Our vocation is students! Only the third definition of vocation is "big enough," I submit, to accommodate the monumental responsibilities that are ours in working with students.

Let me bring these observations to an end by suggesting two

approaches that might be used on campuses to assure that students will indeed be "the objects of our affections"—that they will receive the measure and the kinds of attention that will help them to be and to become their best. The first is somewhat of a compromise in which there is recognition of the importance of students in the academic enterprise and there is provision for a number of selected "student oriented" faculty and staff personnel to give attention to students and their needs. It's an approach with some merit, but it suffers from the standpoint that students in such a program are oftentimes dealt with segmentally with little or no assurance that essential assistance in helping them to achieve an integrated, total experience will be provided. In such an approach, only those faculty, staff, and administrators so inclined, or specifically assigned, work with students. The others "do their own thing," with little or no regard for students. There are those who argue that in today's comprehensive, multi-purpose institutions of higher education, such an approach is both realistic and the best for which we can hope. I hear what they are saying; and I'm grateful for their concern.

I believe there is a better alternative, however—one to which I have already alluded. I favor an approach that aims at achieving a measure of commitment to and involvement with students by everyone who serves in the academic community, recognizing (as has been indicated) that in some faculty, administrative, and staff roles, opportunities to serve students will be limited. Because of the special role of students in higher education, every "senior scholar"—be he or she an administrator, a faculty member, or a member of the staff—needs to "get into the act" to some degree. No one should be so busy with any competing responsibility that the importance of students is dismissed. Albert Einstein stated it well when he observed, "The concern for man and his destiny must always be the chief interest of all technical effort. Never forget it among all your diagrams and equations."

The second approach, it seems to me, holds greater promise for achieving our educational goals and preserving the integrity of the overall educational mission than does the first. It's an approach that can help faculty, administrators, and staff to achieve a genuine sense of community, as together all (rather than only some) give their attentions and affections to students. And from the standpoint of students, it's the more desirable of the two approaches, for there is the greater possibility of their being dealt with totally, rather than on a piece-meal basis. Knowing that all faculty, staff, and administrators share an interest in them (rather than only a few selected ones) can do wonders for them as they seek "to be and to become."

How can we achieve the second of the two approaches? How can we get some measure of involvement with students on the parts of all administrators, faculty, and staff? First of all there must be achieved a commitment on the parts of those in the academic community (beginning with the president who must provide the leadership for the achievement of such), relative to the importance of students in the academic endeavor. There must be conversation and communication among all members of the faculty, administration, and staff relative to what is entailed in such a commitment, as well as to how it can be realized. Both persistence and patience will be necessary, for the achievement of a campus climate in which the students truly are "the objects of our affections" will take time. It's a process, not an event. A presidential pronouncement alone will not suffice.

Once there is a good measure of commitment on the parts of those who teach students in classrooms and laboratories, as well as those who work with students in various out-of-class activities, new and exciting opportunities to be of service to students will begin to become evident. The receptionist, the teacher, the residence hall counselor, and those in the many other roles on campus will soon discover additional ways to help students to achieve their best.

In working with students, our task is largely one of helping them discover who they are—intellectually, physically, socially, emotionally, and spiritually. Because every student is an individual, it's something that cannot be done on a mass-production basis. Committed faculty, staff, and administrators will view every student contact as an opportunity to assist the student—not to "spoon-feed" him or her, but to help that person to assume the responsibilities of young adulthood. We deal with individuals, however, and some will need more direct assistance than will others. Some, in fact, will need to learn how to walk before they can run. Those sensitive to the welfare of students will recognize the differences in students' needs, and assist accordingly.

For most students, the early identification of an appropriate career goal (or some alternative possibilities) can be a factor in helping them to discover who they are, and where they are going.

Finally, I would underscore that, whereas different individuals require different amounts of time and different kinds of assistance in serving their needs and resolving their problems, all students need to know of our affection. To assure all students (both the lovely and the unlovely), through our words and actions, that they are loved—that they indeed are "the objects of our affections"—will go a long way in helping each to realize his or her full potential—which really is a mighty important part of the total mission of higher education!

A Chronological Listing
of References
Presented with deep appreciation and thanks

In presenting reference materials for *The Best of Mind and Spirit*, a chronological listing is provided. The references and their respective identifying numbers follow:

(1)   Kershner, Frederick, Jr., *DeToqueville's America—The Great Quotations*. Ohio University Press, Athens, London. Commissioned and funded by Cooper Industries.

(2)   Whitman, Walt, *Leaves of Grass*. Garden City, N.Y.: Double Day and Company, 1964 edited version by Emory Holloway, Editor.

(3)   Kellogg Commission on the Future of State and Land-Grant Universities, E. Gordon Gee, Chairman. *Returning to our Roots—The Student Experience*. Washington, D. C.: National Association of State Universities and Land-Grant Colleges, 1997.

(4)   Committee on Student Personnel Work, E. G. Williamson, Chairman. *The Student Personnel Point of View* (rev. ed.). American Council on Education Studies, Series VI, No. 13. Washington, D. C., 1949.

(5)   Bresler, Wendy, Editor-in-Chief. "College and Character: Preparing Students for Lives of Civic Responsibility." *Educational Record: The Magazine of Higher Education*, Summer/Fall, 1997.

(6)   Wolfe, Thomas, *You Can't Go Home Again*. New York: Perennial Library, 1973, Harper and Row, Publishers.

(7)   Fund, John, "Politics, Economics, and Education in the 21st Century." *IMPRIMIS* (the monthly journal of Hillsdale College). Reprinted by permission of *IMPRIMIS*, May, 1998.

(8)   Bork, Robert H., *Slouching Towards Gomorrah*. New York: Regan Books, Harper-Collins Publishers, Inc., 1996.

(9)   Leo, John, "A No Fault Holocaust." *U.S. News and World Report*, July 21, 1997.

(10) Colson, Charles and Pearcey, Nancy, "Poster Boy for Postmodernism." *Christianity Today*, November 16, 1998.

(11) Mandelbaum, Bernard, *Choose Life*. New York: Random House, 1968.

(12) Mill, John as quoted in Mandelbaum, Bernard, *Choose Life* (11).

(13) Cooley, Ralph, "Still on Campus, After All These Years." *Worldwide Challenge* (Campus Crusade for Christ Magazine). September/October, 1997.

(14) Willimon, William H., "Religious Faith and the Development of Character on Campus," as presented in *The Educational Record*, Summer/Fall, 1997 (5).

(15) Marsden, George, *The Soul of the American University: From Protestant Establishment to Established Nonbelief*. New York: Oxford University Press, 1994.

(16) Brown, Kenneth Irving, *Not Minds Alone*. New York: Harper and Brothers, 1954.

(17) Peterson, Duane, Oklahoma State University Anatomy Regents Professor Emeritus: Comments on the creation-evolution issue, April 8, 1998.

(18) Fuhlendorf, Sam, Oklahoma State University Department of Plant and Soil Science Professor: Comments on "The

Dichotomy of Evolution", April 14, 1999.

(19) Breazile, James, Oklahoma State University Professor of Physiology, and holder of a Masters Degree in theology: Comments on science and religion, May, 1999

(20) Yates, Kyle, long-time holder of the Phoebe Schertz Young Chair in Religious Studies, Head Emeritus of the Oklahoma State University Department of Religious Studies, and an active archeologist: Comments on science and religion, February, 2001.

(21) Christian Defense Fund, Benjamin Hart, President. *One Nation Under God*. Springfield, Virginia, 1997.

(22) Adams, John, as quoted in *One Nation Under God* (21), February 22, 1756.

(23) Adams, John, as quoted in *One Nation Under God* (21), July 3, 1776.

(24) Adams, Samuel, as quoted in *One Nation Under God* (21), 1772.

(25) Adams, Samuel, as quoted in *One Nation Under God* (21), 1776.

(26) Adams, Samuel (In his Last Will and Testament), as quoted in *One Nation Under God* (21).

(27) The Continental Congress: Various actions taken, as reported in *One Nation Under God* (21), including a Proclamation for a Day of Public Thanksgiving and Prayer.

(28) President George Washington's Proclamation of a National Day of Thanksgiving, as reported in *One Nation Under God* (21), (pp. 66, 67).

(29) Basler, Roy P., *Collected Works of Abraham Lincoln*. New Brunswick, New Jersey: Rutgers University Press, 1953, (with supplement, 1974).

(30) The Continental Congress, Declaration of Independence, as reported in *One Nation Under God* (21), July 4, 1776.

(31) Franklin, Benjamin (from his autobiography), as quoted in *One Nation Under God* (21).

(32) Franklin, Benjamin (in a letter of March, 1778, to the Ministry of France), as quoted in *One Nation Under God* (21).

(33) Franklin, Benjamin (in a plea on June 28, 1787) to the delegates to the Constitutional Convention), as quoted in *One Nation Under God* (21).

(34) Hamilton, Alexander (shortly after the Constitutional Convention of 1787), as quoted in *One Nation Under God* (21).

(35) Henry, Patrick (a five-time Governor of Virginia), as quoted in *One Nation Under God* (21).

(36) Henry, Patrick (with reference to the Bible), as quoted in *One Nation Under God* (21).

(37) Madison, James (known as the father of the U.S. Constitution), as quoted in *One Nation Under God* (21).

(38) Madison, James (relative to his Christian faith), as quoted in *One Nation Under God* (21).

(39) Madison, James (relative to his belief in God as all powerful, wise, and good), as quoted in *One Nation Under God* (21).

(40) Lincoln, Abraham (on the occasion of receiving a Bible from the Committee of Colored People from Baltimore, Maryland, September 5, 1864), as quoted in *One Nation Under God* (21).

(41) Whitman, David, "Was It Good For Us?" *U.S. News and World Report*, May 19, 1997.

(42) McManus, Michael, *Marriage Savers*. Grand Rapids, Michigan: Zondervan Publishing House, 1995.

(43)   McHugh, James, the Bishop of Camden, N. J., as reported in the David Whitman article (41).

(44)   Salter, Stephanie, "Could Sex Education Be Working?" *The San Francisco Examiner*, November, 1997.

(45)   Mathewes-Green, Frederica, "Wanted: A New Pro-Life Strategy." *Christianity Today*, January 12, 1998.

(46)   Thompson, J. J., "Plugging the Kegs." *U.S. News and World Report*, January 26, 1998.

(47)   McCaffrey, Barry (USA drug policy adviser), *Associated Press Release*, August 31, 1997.

(48)   Commission on Substance Abuse Among America's Adolescents, *Associated Press Release*, August, 1997.

(49)   Califano, Joseph (former USA Secretary of Health, Education, and Welfare), *Associated Press Release* (NBC's Today Show), August, 1997.

(50)   Horatio Alger Association, "The State of Our Nation's Youth." *Associated Press Release*, August 11, 1998.

(51)   *Tulsa World* (lead editorial), "Child Criminals." August 17, 1998.

(52)   Trout, Paul A., "Incivility in the Classroom Breeds 'Education Lite.'" *The Chronicle of Higher Education*, July 24, 1998.

(53)   Trueblood, David Elton, *Philosophy of Religion*. New York: Harper and Brothers, Publisher, 1957.

(54)   Galloway, George, *Studies in the Philosophy of Religion*. International Theological Library Series, Edinburgh: T and T Clark (Reprint, 1966).

(55)   Temple, William, *Nature, Man, and God*. Gifford Lectures, University of Glasgow, 1932-33 and 1933-34.

(56) Blake, Bruce P., Bishop, Oklahoma Methodist Area, "Spirituality Is All Encompassing." *United Methodist Review*, March 5, 1999.

(57) Sarnoff, David, as quoted in Mandelbaum, Bernard, *Choose Life* (11).

(58) Mather, Kirtley F., *Science in Search of God*. New York: Henry Holt and Company, 1928.

(59) Mather, Kirtley F., *Crusade For Life*. Chapel Hill: The University of North Carolina Press, 1949.

(60) Murrow, Edward R. (Morgan, Edward P., Editor), *This I Believe*. New York: Simon and Schuster, 1952.

(61) Hoover, Herbert, President of the United States of America, 1929-1933, as quoted in Murrow, Edward R., *This I Believe* (60).

(62) Maritain, Jacque, French philosopher and diplomat (and a devout Catholic), as quoted in Brown, Kenneth Irving, *Not Minds Alone* (16).

(63) Lowry, Howard, *The Mind's Adventure*. Philadelphia: Westminster Press, 1950.

(64) Chambers, Oswald, *My Utmost For His Highest*. New York: Dodd, Mead and Company, Inc., 1935.

(65) Simpson, Victor L., "Pope Defend's Church's Values." *Associated Press Release*, the *Tulsa World*, October 16, 1998.

(66) Gandhi, Mahatma, as quoted in Mandelbaum, Bernard, *Choose Life* (11).

(67) Walter, Erich A., Editor, *Religion and the State University*. Ann Arbor: The University of Michigan Press, 1958.

(68) Bean, Walton, "What Is the State University?", as presented in *Religion and the State University* (67).

(69)   Kauper, Paul, "Law and the Public Opinion," as presented in *Religion and the State University* (67).

(70)   White, Helen, "What Place Has Religion in State University Education?" as presented in *Religion and the State University* (67).

(71)   Ingraham, Mark H., "Academic Freedom," as presented in *Religion and the State University* (67).

(72)   Shuster, George, "Religion and the Professions," as presented in *Religion and the State University* (67).

(73)   "Report of the National Consultative Conference on Religion and the State University," *Religious Education*, official publication of the Religious Education Association, 545 West 11st Street, New York 25, N. Y. March/April, 1959.

(74)   Moberly, Sir Walter, *The Crisis in the University*. London: SCM Press, 1949.

(3)   Kellogg Commission on the Future of State and Land-Grant Universities, E. Gordon Gee, Chairman, *Access.* Washington, D. C., National Association of State Universities and Land-Grant Colleges, 1998.

(75)   Campbell, John R., *Reclaiming a Lost Heritage . . . Land-Grant and Other Higher Education Initiatives for the Twenty-First Century*. East Lansing, Michigan: Michigan State University Press, 1998.

(4)   Zook, George F., President of the American Council on Education, "Foreword," *The Student Personnel Point of View*, June 1, 1949 (4).

(76)   Dalton, John C. and Petrie, Anne Marie, "The Power of Peer Culture," as presented in *The Educational Record*, Summer/Fall, 1997 (5).

(77)   American Council on Education Report of ACE Task

Force regarding "Strategies to Reduce Alcohol Abuse," in its publication entitled *Higher Education and National Affairs*, Washington, D. C., September 14, 1998 (77).

(78) Menninger, Karl, *Whatever Became of Sin?* New York: Hawthorn Books, 1973.

(79) St. Francis of Assisi: (Born of wealth in 1182, Francis disavowed all property and a life of ease in favor of serving the poor and the suffering. In 1812 the Pope authorized an Order of Friars Minor, commonly called the Franciscans. St. Francis died in 1226.)

(80) Cousins, Norman, as quoted in Mandelbaum, Bernard, *Choose Life* (11).

(81) Stevenson, Adlai E., as quoted in Mandelbaum, Bernard, *Choose Life* (11).

(82) Buber, Martin, as quoted in Mandelbaum, Bernard, *Choose Life* (11).

(83) Report of the work of Kathleen and Chris Macosko with international students at the University of Minnesota, entitled "The World at Our Doorstep." *The Real Issue*, September/October, 1997.

(84) Federer, William J., *America's God and Country Encyclopedia of Quotations*. Coppell, Texas: Fame Publishing, Inc., 1994.

(85) Jefferson, Thomas, "Prayer For Peace," as quoted in Federer's *America's God and Country Encyclopedia of Quotations* (84).

(86) Jefferson, Thomas, "Notes on the State of Virginia," as quoted in *One Nation Under God* (21).

(87) Garrett, Sandy, as reported in *The Daily Oklahoman*, July 22, 1998.

(88) Wilson, David and Ruth Ann, "Teaching Positive Values in

the Classroom." *Delta Kappa Gamma Bulletin*, Summer, 1997.

(89)   Clark, Power R. and Lapsley, Daniel, Editors, *The Challenge of Pluralism: Education, Politics, and Values.* Notre Dame, Indiana: University of Notre Dame Press, 1992.

(90)   Gabrels, Sara Terry, "The Age of Casting No Stones." *The Christian Science Monitor*, February 18, 1998.

(91)   Kamm, Robert B., Review of *The College Influence on Student Character* by Eddy, Edward D., *Faculty Forum*, Division of Educational Institutions, the Methodist Church and the Board of Education of the Presbyterian Church, U.S., October, 1959.

(92)   Eddy, Edward D., *The College Influence on Student Character.* Washington, D. C.: The American Council on Education, 1959.

(93)   Groome, Thomas H., "...And Infuse Education with More Spiritual Values." *The Christian Science Monitor*, February 10, 1998.

(94)   Groome, Thomas H., *Educating For Life: A Spiritual Vision for Every Teacher and Parent.* Allen, Texas: Thomas More Publishing, 1998.

(95)   Bennett, William J., "Revolt Against God—America's Spiritual Despair."[d] *The Heritage Association's Policy Review*, Winter, 1994.

(96)   Burns, James MacGregor, *Leadership.* Harper Colophon Books: Harper and Row Publishers, 1978.

(97)   Kamm, Robert B., *Leadership For Leadership, Number One Priority for Presidents and Other Administrators.* Washington, D. C.: University Press of America, Inc., 1982. (Second Printing, Stillwater, OK: New Forums Press, Inc., 1988.)

(98)   Seabourn, Keith, (Director of Internet Development, Christian Leadership Ministries), *Telling the Truth on the*

Internet: A "How To" Guide. Carrollton, Texas: May 12, 1998.

(99) Mathewes-Green, Frederica, "Character Does Matter." *The Real Issue*, September/ October, 1998.

(100) Collins, Judy, *Amazing Grace.* New York: Hyperion, 1991.

(101) Smallwood, James, *And Gladly Teach.* Norman: University of Oklahoma Press, 1976.

(102) Highet, Gilbert, *The Art of Teaching.* New York: Knopf, 1950.

(103) Spanier, Graham, "Information Technology's Impact on Higher Education." *NASULGC Newsline*, February, 1998.

(104) McGrath, C. Peter, in his *NASULGC Newsletter*, September 4, 1998.

(105) Briggs, David, *Religion News Service*, "Want to Live a Longer Life? Then Go to Church on Sunday, Researchers Say." *The Daily Oklahoman*, December 10, 1998.

(106) Halverson, Chris, Editor, *Perspective Letter.* Concern Ministries, McClean, Virginia: September, 1997.

(107) Kamm, Robert B., "Our Vocation Is Students." Address presented to the March, 1959 meeting of the National Association of Women Deans and Counselors, Washington, D. C.

(108) Michalson, Carl, *Faith For Personal Crises.* New York: Scribner, 1958.

(109) Raspberry, William, "Rediscovering the Power of the Spirit." *The Denver Post*, December 25, 1992.

(110) Holman, Nat, "You Cannot 'Fix' a Faith," as quoted in Morgan, Edward P., *This I Believe* (60).

(111) Mother Teresa, *Meditations From a Simple Path.* New York: Ballantine Books, 1996.

(112) Mellichamp, Rae, "How to Restore Christian Thought in the University." *The Real Issue*, September/October, 1997.

(113) Harris, Edward L., "Toward Integrating Your Life and Your Work." *The Real Issue*, January 2, 1997.

(114) Johnson, Benita, "Letter to the Editor." *The Stillwater News-Press*, July 12, 1998.

(115) Jerden, Larry, "Bringing the Good News to America's School Children." *American Bible Society Record*, February/March, 1998.

(116) Schneider, Allison, "Jane Tompkin's Message to Academe: Nurture the Individual, Not Just the Intellect." *The Chronicle of Higher Education*, July 10, 1998.

(117) Hawkes, Herbert E. and Hawkes, Anna L. Rose, *Through a Dean's Open Door*. New York: McGraw-Hill Book Company, Inc., 1945 (117), (p. v of Introduction).

(118) Kamm, Robert B., "Quality Teaching in Higher Education." *The Oklahoma Teacher*, April, 1963.

(119) Dirks, J. Edward, "Higher Education and Christian Conscience." *The Christian Scholar,* Winter, 1960.

(120) Fagan, Patrick F., "The Real Root Cause of Violent Crime." *IMPRIMIS* (the monthly journal of Hillsdale College), October, 1995.[d]

(121) Horn, Wade F., "Why There Is No Substitute for Parents." *IMPRIMIS* (the monthly journal of Hillsdale College), June 1, 1997.(d)

(122) Gregory, Neal, "Keeping America's Promise—Powell-Led Army Mobilizing to Help At-Risk Youth." National Retired Teachers Association, *NRTA Bulletin*, April, 1999.

(123) Oklahoma United Methodist Church, Circle of Care, Inc., Tom Campbell, Executive Director, 2420 N. Blackwelder,

Oklahoma City, OK 73106-1499.

(124) Trueheart, Charles, "Welcome to the Next Church." *The Atlantic Monthly*, August, 1996.

(125) Presbyterian Board of Christian Education, *The Hymnal.* Philadelphia: Published by Authority of the General Assembly of the Presbyterian Church of the United States of America, 1933.

(126) Bowdon, Boyce A., *The Child Friendly Church.* Nashville: Abingdon Press, 1999.

(127) McGrath, C. Peter, Letter to the Leadership of the National Association of State Universities and Land-Grant Colleges, June 1, 1998.

(128) National Panhellenic Conference, U-WIRE report regarding resolution "endorsing substance-free fraternities, and encouraging their 26 member sororities to participate in alcohol-free events with them." Evanston, Ill., October 17, 1998.

(129) U-WIRE out of State College, Pennsylvania regarding Pennsylvania State Law, Act 199, effective February 18, 1998 (includes restrictions on advertising alcoholic beverages in campus publications).

(130) Shalala, Donna E., Secretary, United States Health and Human Resources. Address regarding "the need to cut ties between college athletics and drinking." National Collegiate Athletic Association Convention, January 12, 1998.

(131) Crowley, Susan L., "Minow's Long Campaign to Improve TV for Kids." National Retired Teachers Association, *NRTA Bulletin*, May, 1998.

(132) Baker, Jimmie, a veteran of more than 50 years with ABC Television, and the retired head of Jamie Productions.

(133) Browning, Robert, "Pippo's Song." *English Literature and Background, Revised Edition, Volume 2.* Grebanier, Bernard; Middlebrook, Samuel; Thompson, Stith; and Watt, William. New York: The Dryden Press, 1940.

(134) Schuller, Robert, "In God We Still Trust." *The American Legion Magazine*, September, 1997.

(135) Toynbee, Arnold and Ikeda, Daisaku, *Choose Life—A Dialogue*, Edited by Richard L. Gage. London: Oxford University Press, 1976.

(136) Kamm, Robert B., "The Need For Talent in All Worthwhile Labor." *The Oklahoma Teacher*, September, 1963. (Appendix C).

(137) Kamm, Robert B., "Our Vocation Is Students." *Journal of the National Association of Women Deans and Counselors*, October, 1959. (Appendix D).

(138) Kamm, Robert B., "Restoration in Discipline." *The Personnel and Guidance Journal*, May, 1955. (Appendix E).

(139) Kamm, Robert B., "The Management of Conflict." Unpublished address presented to the General Council of Omicron Delta Kappa, National Leadership Fraternity, at its 1972 convention at Cleveland, Ohio. (Appendix F).

(140) Kamm, Robert B., "The Object of My Affection." Unpublished paper prepared for, and presented to, older, non-traditional students enrolled in the writer's doctoral level courses, 1980. (Appendix G).

(141) Michalson, Carl. *Faith for Personal Crises*. New York: Charles Scribner's Sons, 1958.

(142) Brown, Kenneth I. *Not Mind's Alone*. New York: Harper and Brothers, 1954.

(143) Moberly, Sir Walter. *The Crisis in the University*. London: SCM Press, 1949.

(144) Lowry, Howard. *The Mind's Adventure.* Philadelphia: Westminster Press, 1950.

(145) Cousins, Norman. *In God We Trust.* New York: Harper and Brothers, 1958.

(146) Cuninggim, Merrimon. *The College Seeks Religion.* New Haven: Yale University Press, 1947.

(147) Calhoun, Robert L. "The Place of Religion in Higher Education." *The Hazen Pamphlets, No. 2.* New Haven: The Edward W. Hazen Foundation.

(148) Livingstone, Sir Richard. "Some Thoughts on University Education." *The Hazen Pamphlets, No. 23.* New Haven: The Edward W. Hazen Foundation.

(149) Committee on Student Personnel Work, E. G. Williamson, Chairman. *The Student Personnel Point of View* (rev. ed.). American Council on Education Studies, Series VI, No. 13. American Council on Education, Washington, 1949, 20 pp.

(150) Hawkes, Herbert E. and Hawkes, Anna L. Rose, *Through a Dean's Open Door.* New York, McGraw-Hill Book Company, Inc., 1945, 242 pp.

(151) Lloyd-Jones, Esther and Smith, Margaret Ruth, *Student Personnel Work as Deeper Teaching.* New York, Harper and Brothers, 1954, 361 pp.

(152) Wrenn, C. Gilbert, *Student Personnel Work in College.* New York, The Ronald Press Company, 1951, 589 pp.

(153) Williamson, E. G. and Foley, J. D., *Counseling and Discipline.* New York, McGraw-Hill Book Company, Inc., 1949, 387 pp.

(154) Paton, Alan, *Too Late the Phalarope.* New York, Charles Scribner's Sons, 1953.

Endnotes

(a)   As used in *The Best of Mind and Spirit*, "public schools" and "public education" refer generally to all of public education, pre-school through doctoral study. On occasion, however, references are made to "higher education" only—not to exclude other levels of public education, but because it has been in higher education where the author has served most of his professional life, and from which he can draw upon personal experience most readily.

(b)   The designation "America" or "USA" will usually be used in place of "The United States of America."

(c)   In the Book of Amos of the Old Testament of the Bible, Gotells the prophet Amos, "Behold, I will set a plumbline in the midst of my people Israel" (Amos 7:8, KJV). Though there are many excellent modern translations of the Bible, the King James Version (KJV) continues to be the most widely accepted version, and therefore a decision has been made to refer to it when quoting from the Bible.

(d)   Reprinted by permission of *IMPRIMIS*.

(e)   *Choose Life* (11) is a magnificent presentation by Rabbi Bernard Mandelbaum of expressions of "the best of mind and spirit" through the ages by people from throughout the world—a storehouse of wisdom for living the good life.

(f)   I digress for the moment from referring primarily to what is happening to public institutions to what is also happening at some church-founded and privately supported institutions.

(g)   Published with permission of the Christian Defense Fund, Benjamin Hart, President.

(h)   Printed with the permission of the author and/or publisher.

(i)   Based on the abbreviated version of the survey conducted by the Luntz Research Cos.

(j)   *This I Believe* (60) is another storehouse of wisdom in which examples of "the best of mind and spirit" are shared in the literature.

(k)   As a junior high school boy in Iowa during President Hoover's term of office, I came to love and to respect OUR courageous President during those difficult years for America.

(l)   Published with permission of the University of Michigan Press.

(m)   Through the years, I have published articles and presented talks that have reflected varied influences on my life. Appendix C, an article entitled "The Need for Talent in All Worthwhile Labor," which appeared in the September 1963 issue of *The Oklahoma Teacher*, the publication of the Oklahoma Education Association, reflects the Land-Grant philosophy (136).

(n)   Appendices D and E both reflect the spirit and the application of "the student personnel point of view." Appendix D, entitled "Our Vocation Is Students" (137), is an address presented at the Palm Sunday morning session of the 1959 annual meeting of the National Association of Women Deans and Counselors at Philadelphia, PA. It was later published in the *Journal of the National Association of Women Deans and Counselors*. Appendix E, entitled "Restoration In Discipline" (138), was published in the May 1955 issue of *The Personnel and Guidance Journal*. As the title suggests, the article points to the need for a caring approach in discipline aimed at salvaging those in trouble rather than relying strictly on punitive measures.

(o)   In the KJV, the word "charity" is used synonymously with the word "love."

(p)   The first American astronaut to orbit the earth (1962) and, at the age of 77 (1998), the oldest astronaut to return to space.

(q)   Appendix F entitled "The Management of Conflict" (138), is an address about leadership presented to the General Council of Omicron Delta Kappa, National Leadership Fraternity, at its 1972 Naitonal Convention.

(r)   Reproduced with the permission of the American Bible Society.

(s)   Appendix G entitled, "The Object of My Affection," is an unpublished paper, 1980 (140).

(t)   Reprinted by permission of the author and of the NRTA.

(u)   At the time of completion of this volume, Mr. Powell serves as Secretary of State in the USA cabinet of President George W. Bush.

(v)   Printed with permission of *The Atlantic Monthly*.

(w)   While a distinction often is made between "personal character development" and "civic education" as if the terms were mutually exclusive, Astin stated that he is deliberately integrating the two into what he called development of "civic character."

(x)   Frederica Mathewes-Green was also quoted in Chapter VII from her article entitled "Character Does Matter" (99), published in the September/October 1998 issue of *The Real Issue*.

(y)   Reprinted with permission of the *NRTA Bulletin*.

(z)   Printed by permission of Oxford University Press.

(aa)   Committee on Student Personnel Work, E.G. Williamson, Chairman, *The Student Personnel Point of View* (rev. ed.), American Council on Education Studies, Series VI, No. 13, Washington: American Council on Education, 1949.